HÄGAR

The Great Gour

MUMMY, DOES DADDY STILL LOVE YOU?
ONLY WHEN HE'S HAD ENOUGH TO EAT!

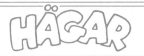

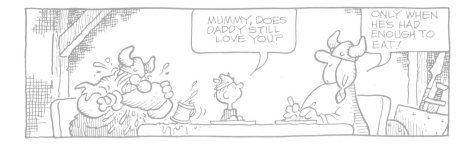

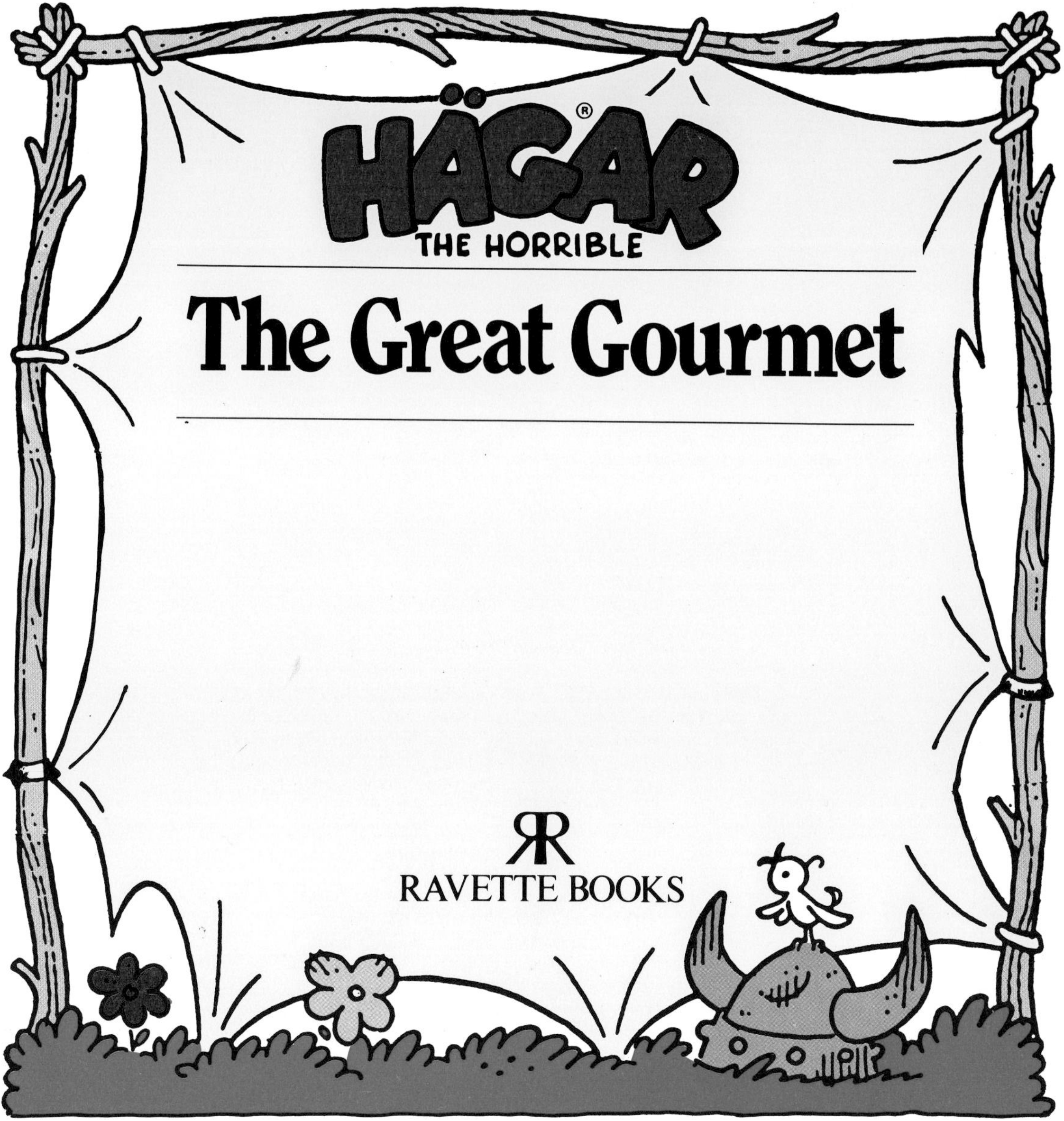

HÄGAR®

THE HORRIBLE

The Great Gourmet

RAVETTE BOOKS

This edition first published by Ravette Books Limited 1989

Printed and Bound
for Ravette Books Limited,
3 Glenside Estate, Star Road, Partridge Green,
Horsham, West Sussex RH13 8RA
by Mateu Cromo Artes Gráfica, s.a.

ISBN: 1 85304 211 0

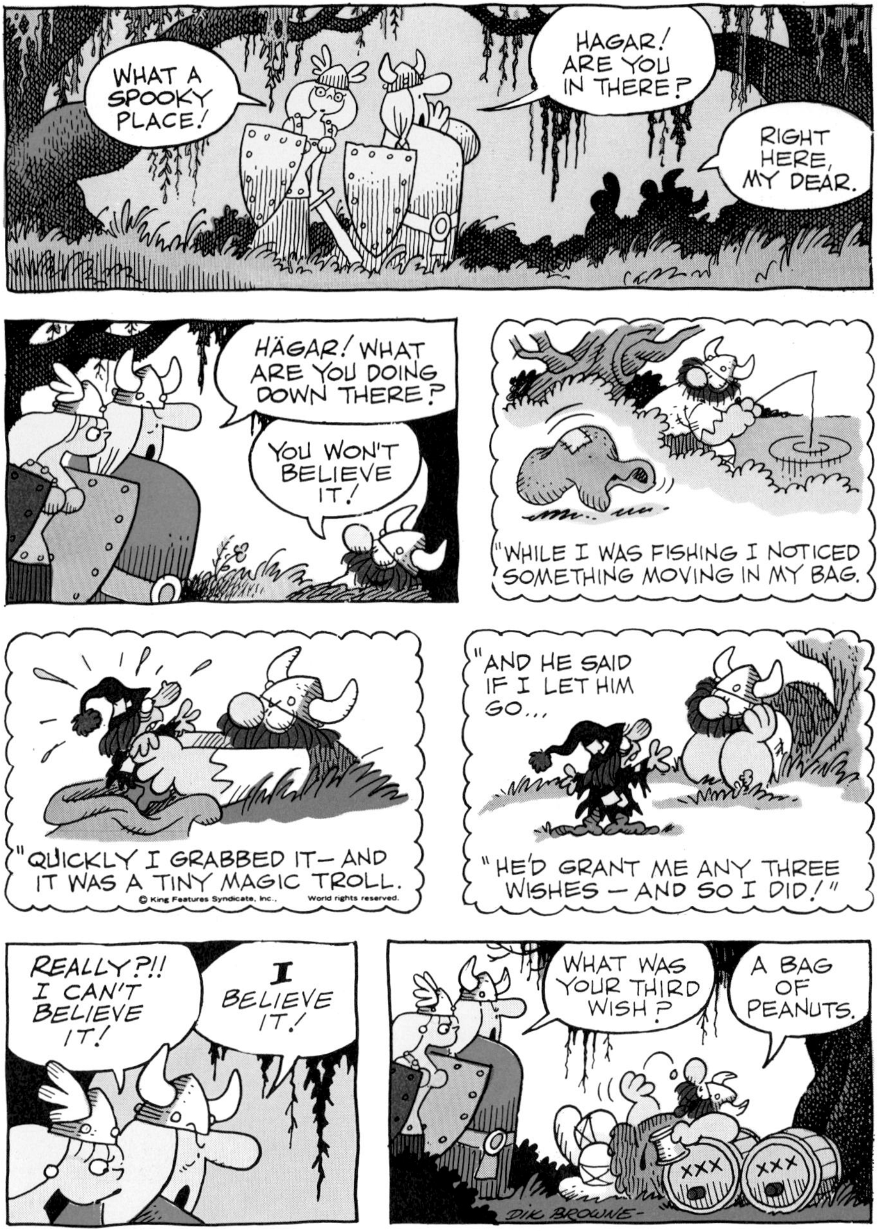
WHAT A SPOOKY PLACE!
HAGAR! ARE YOU IN THERE?
RIGHT HERE, MY DEAR.
HÄGAR! WHAT ARE YOU DOING DOWN THERE?
YOU WON'T BELIEVE IT!
"WHILE I WAS FISHING I NOTICED SOMETHING MOVING IN MY BAG.
"QUICKLY I GRABBED IT— AND IT WAS A TINY MAGIC TROLL.
© King Features Syndicate, Inc., World rights reserved.
"AND HE SAID IF I LET HIM GO...
"HE'D GRANT ME ANY THREE WISHES — AND SO I DID!"
REALLY?!! I CAN'T BELIEVE IT!
I BELIEVE IT!
WHAT WAS YOUR THIRD WISH?
A BAG OF PEANUTS.
XXX
XXX
DIK BROWNE

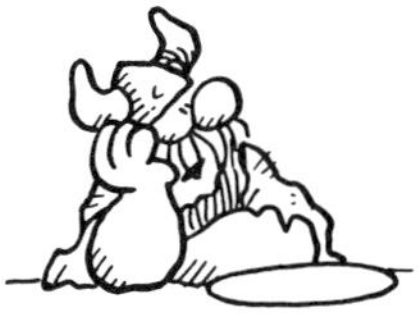

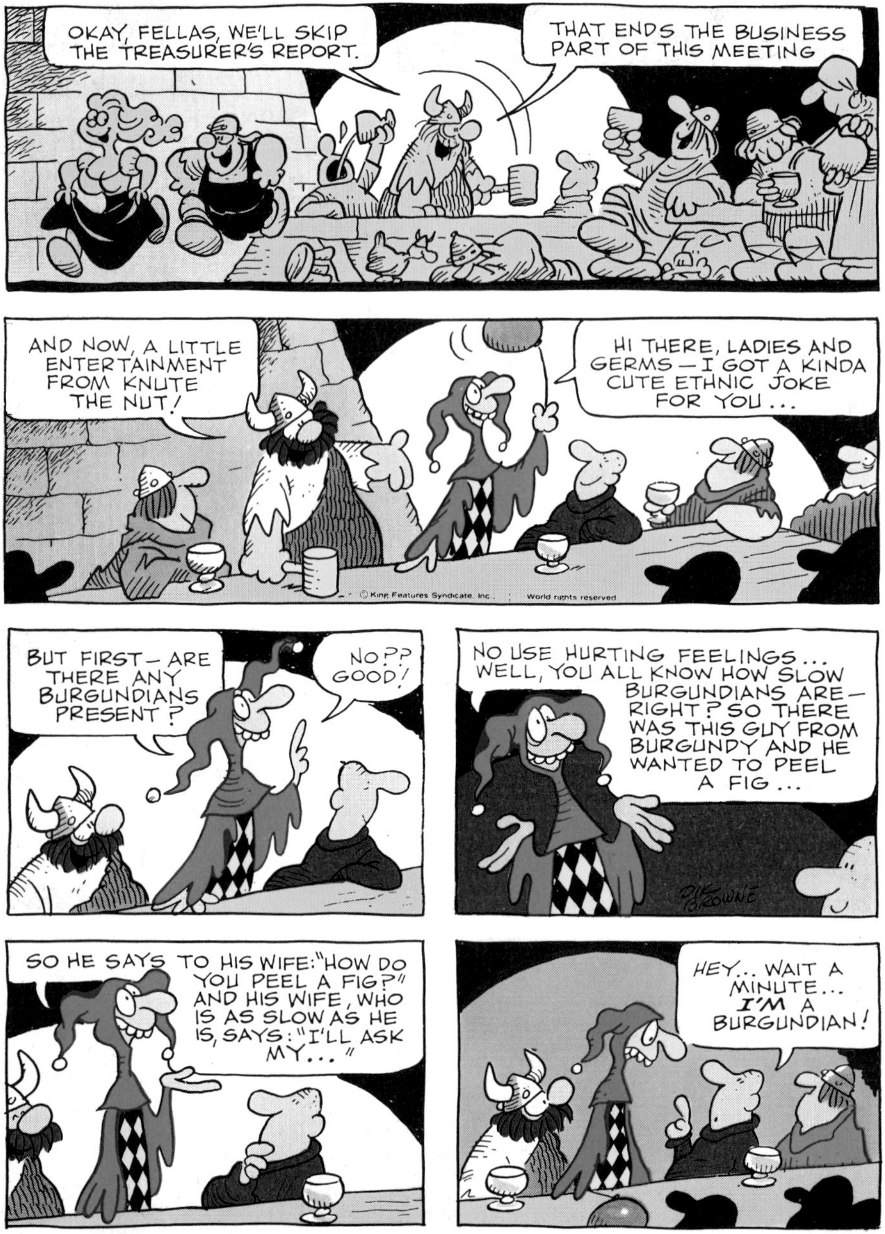

OKAY, FELLAS, WE'LL SKIP THE TREASURER'S REPORT.
THAT ENDS THE BUSINESS PART OF THIS MEETING
AND NOW, A LITTLE ENTERTAINMENT FROM KNUTE THE NUT!
HI THERE, LADIES AND GERMS — I GOT A KINDA CUTE ETHNIC JOKE FOR YOU . . .
© King Features Syndicate, Inc. World rights reserved
BUT FIRST — ARE THERE ANY BURGUNDIANS PRESENT?
NO?? GOOD!
NO USE HURTING FEELINGS . . . WELL, YOU ALL KNOW HOW SLOW BURGUNDIANS ARE — RIGHT? SO THERE WAS THIS GUY FROM BURGUNDY AND HE WANTED TO PEEL A FIG . . .
DIK BROWNE
SO HE SAYS TO HIS WIFE: "HOW DO YOU PEEL A FIG?" AND HIS WIFE, WHO IS AS SLOW AS HE IS, SAYS: "I'LL ASK MY . . ."
HEY . . . WAIT A MINUTE . . . *I'M* A BURGUNDIAN!

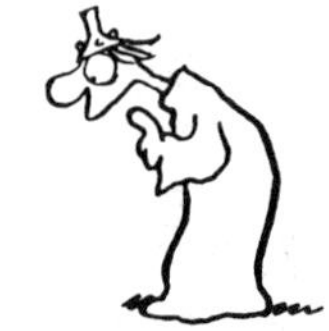

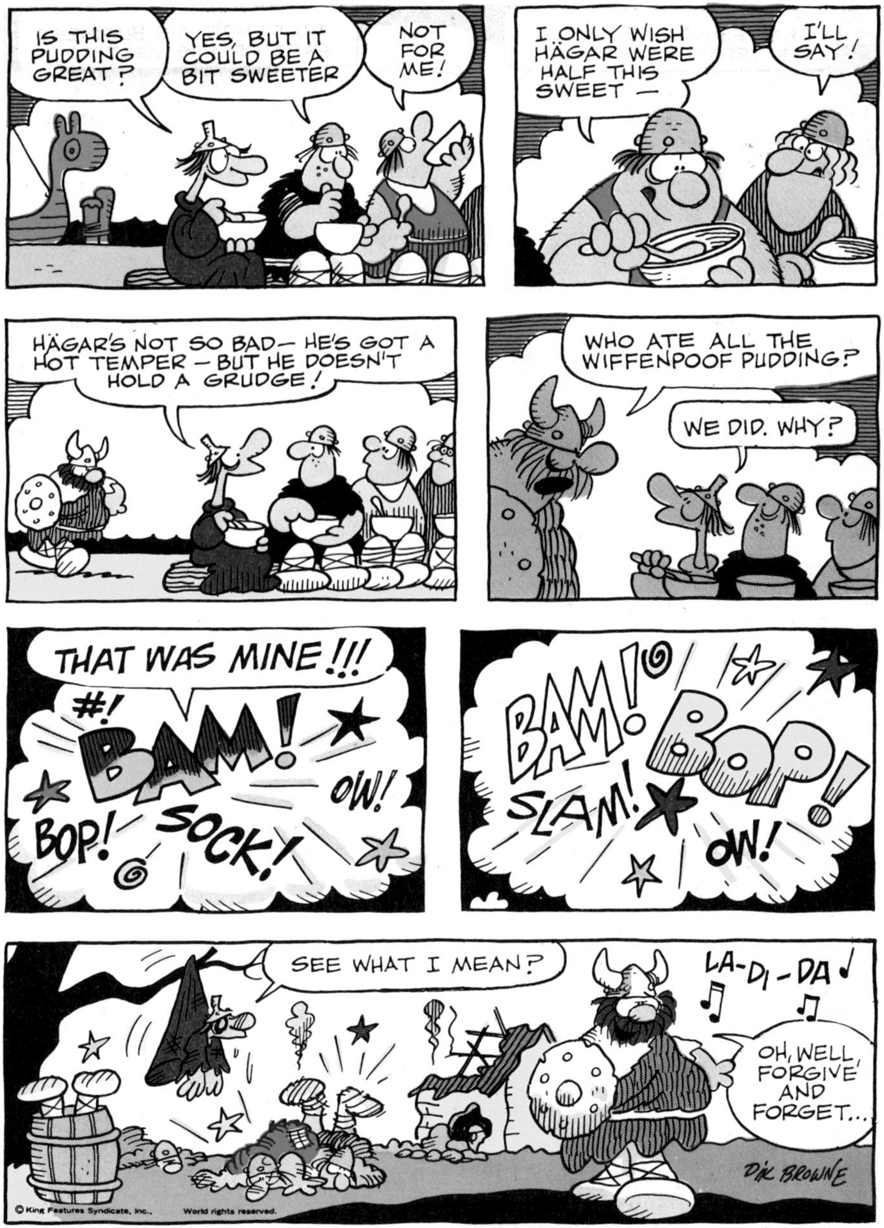
IS THIS PUDDING GREAT?
YES, BUT IT COULD BE A BIT SWEETER
NOT FOR ME!
I ONLY WISH HÄGAR WERE HALF THIS SWEET —
I'LL SAY!
HÄGAR'S NOT SO BAD— HE'S GOT A HOT TEMPER — BUT HE DOESN'T HOLD A GRUDGE!
WHO ATE ALL THE WIFFENPOOF PUDDING?
WE DID. WHY?
THAT WAS MINE!!!
#!
BAM!
OW!
BOP!
SOCK!
BAM!
BOP!
SLAM!
OW!
SEE WHAT I MEAN?
LA-DI-DA
OH, WELL, FORGIVE AND FORGET...
DIK BROWNE
© King Features Syndicate, Inc., World rights reserved.

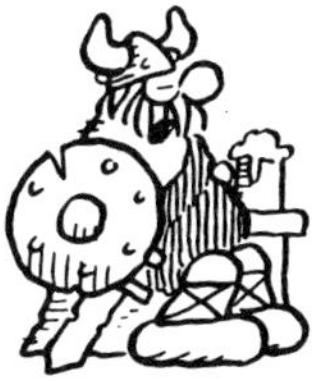

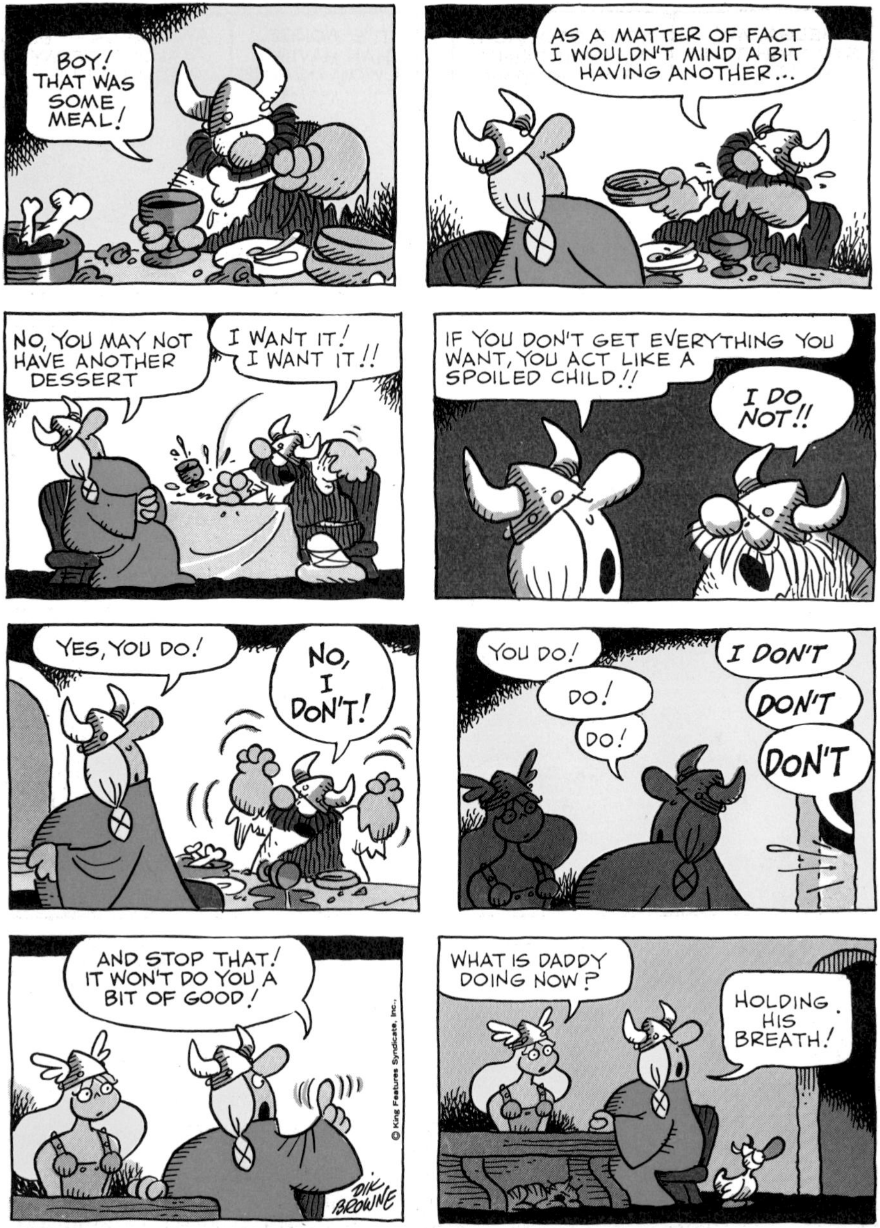
BOY! THAT WAS SOME MEAL!
AS A MATTER OF FACT I WOULDN'T MIND A BIT HAVING ANOTHER...
NO, YOU MAY NOT HAVE ANOTHER DESSERT
I WANT IT! I WANT IT!!
IF YOU DON'T GET EVERYTHING YOU WANT, YOU ACT LIKE A SPOILED CHILD!!
I DO NOT!!
YES, YOU DO!
NO, I DON'T!
YOU DO!
DO!
DO!
I DON'T
DON'T
DON'T
AND STOP THAT! IT WON'T DO YOU A BIT OF GOOD!
© King Features Syndicate, Inc.
DIK BROWNE
WHAT IS DADDY DOING NOW?
HOLDING HIS BREATH!

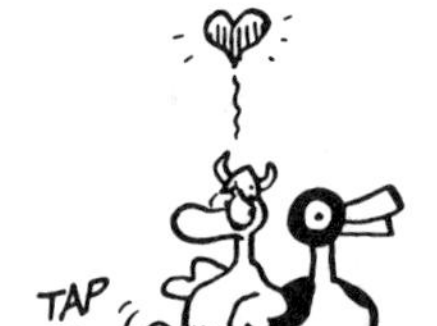
TAP
TAP

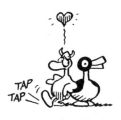

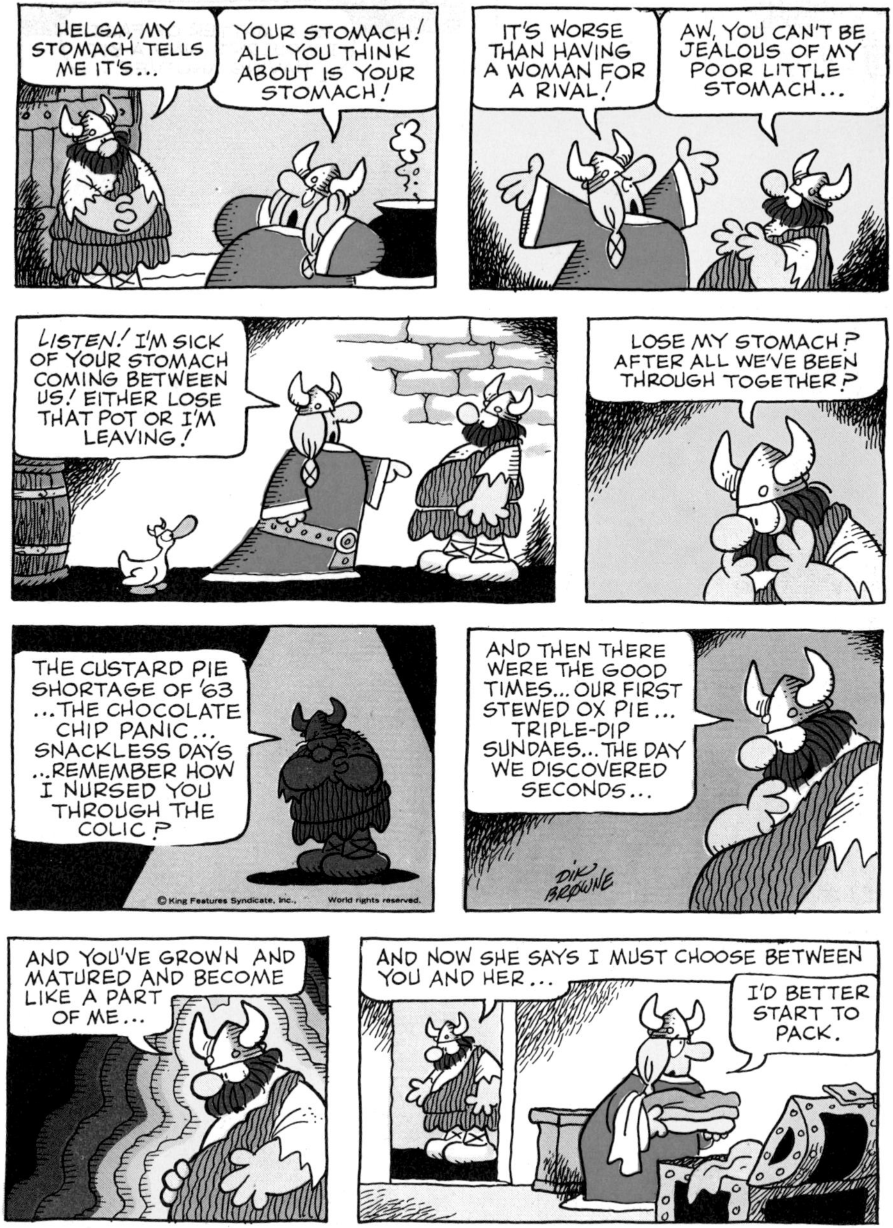
HELGA, MY STOMACH TELLS ME IT'S...
YOUR STOMACH! ALL YOU THINK ABOUT IS YOUR STOMACH!
IT'S WORSE THAN HAVING A WOMAN FOR A RIVAL!
AW, YOU CAN'T BE JEALOUS OF MY POOR LITTLE STOMACH...
LISTEN! I'M SICK OF YOUR STOMACH COMING BETWEEN US! EITHER LOSE THAT POT OR I'M LEAVING!
LOSE MY STOMACH? AFTER ALL WE'VE BEEN THROUGH TOGETHER?
THE CUSTARD PIE SHORTAGE OF '63 ...THE CHOCOLATE CHIP PANIC... SNACKLESS DAYS ...REMEMBER HOW I NURSED YOU THROUGH THE COLIC?
© King Features Syndicate, Inc., World rights reserved.
AND THEN THERE WERE THE GOOD TIMES... OUR FIRST STEWED OX PIE... TRIPLE-DIP SUNDAES... THE DAY WE DISCOVERED SECONDS...
DIK BROWNE
AND YOU'VE GROWN AND MATURED AND BECOME LIKE A PART OF ME...
AND NOW SHE SAYS I MUST CHOOSE BETWEEN YOU AND HER...
I'D BETTER START TO PACK.

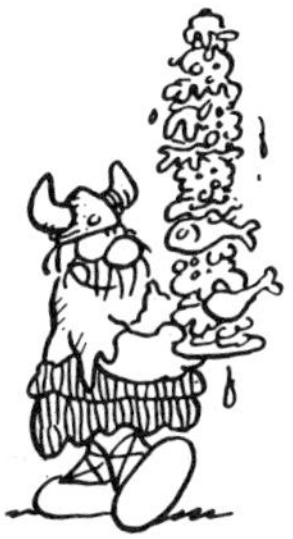

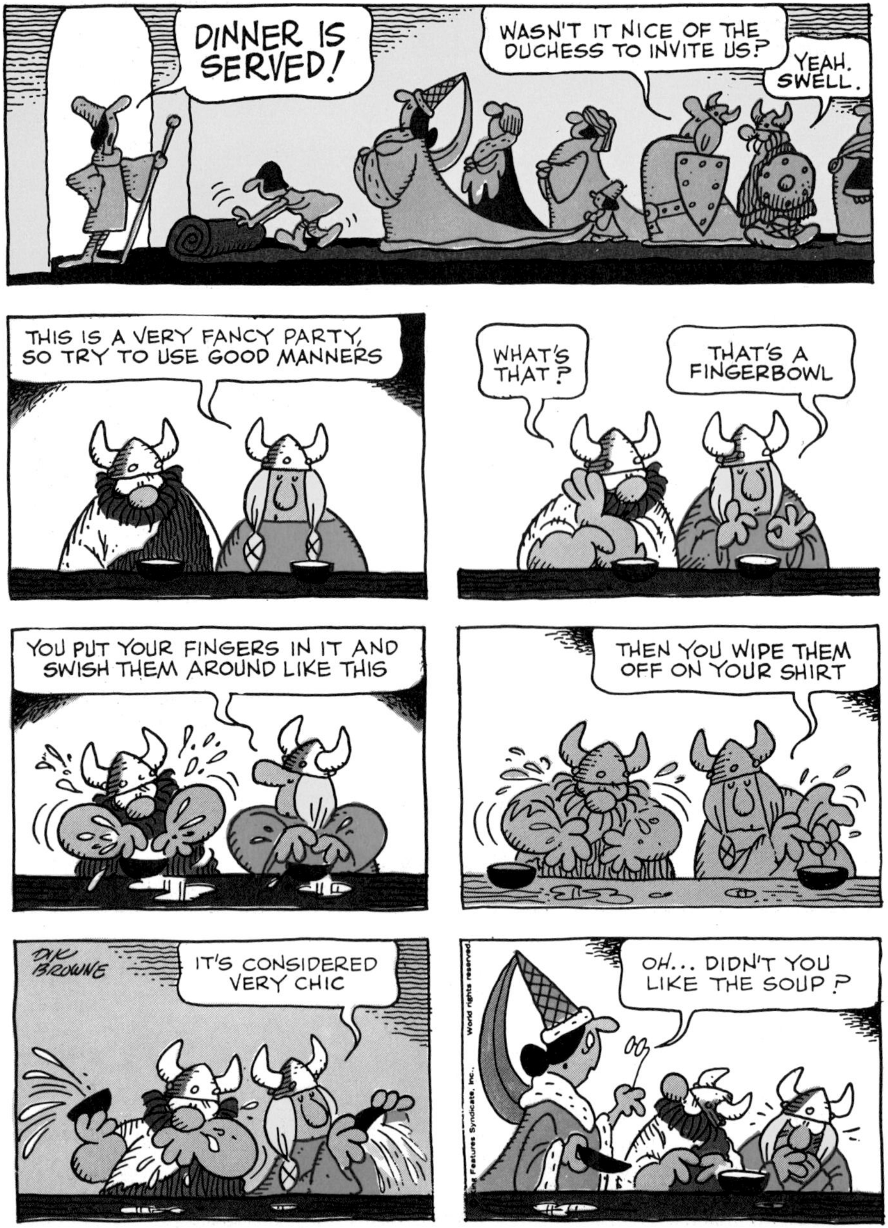

DINNER IS SERVED!
WASN'T IT NICE OF THE DUCHESS TO INVITE US?
YEAH. SWELL.
THIS IS A VERY FANCY PARTY, SO TRY TO USE GOOD MANNERS
WHAT'S THAT?
THAT'S A FINGERBOWL
YOU PUT YOUR FINGERS IN IT AND SWISH THEM AROUND LIKE THIS
THEN YOU WIPE THEM OFF ON YOUR SHIRT
DIK BROWNE
IT'S CONSIDERED VERY CHIC
OH... DIDN'T YOU LIKE THE SOUP?
Features Syndicate, Inc.. World rights reserved.

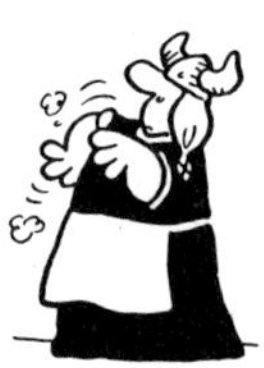

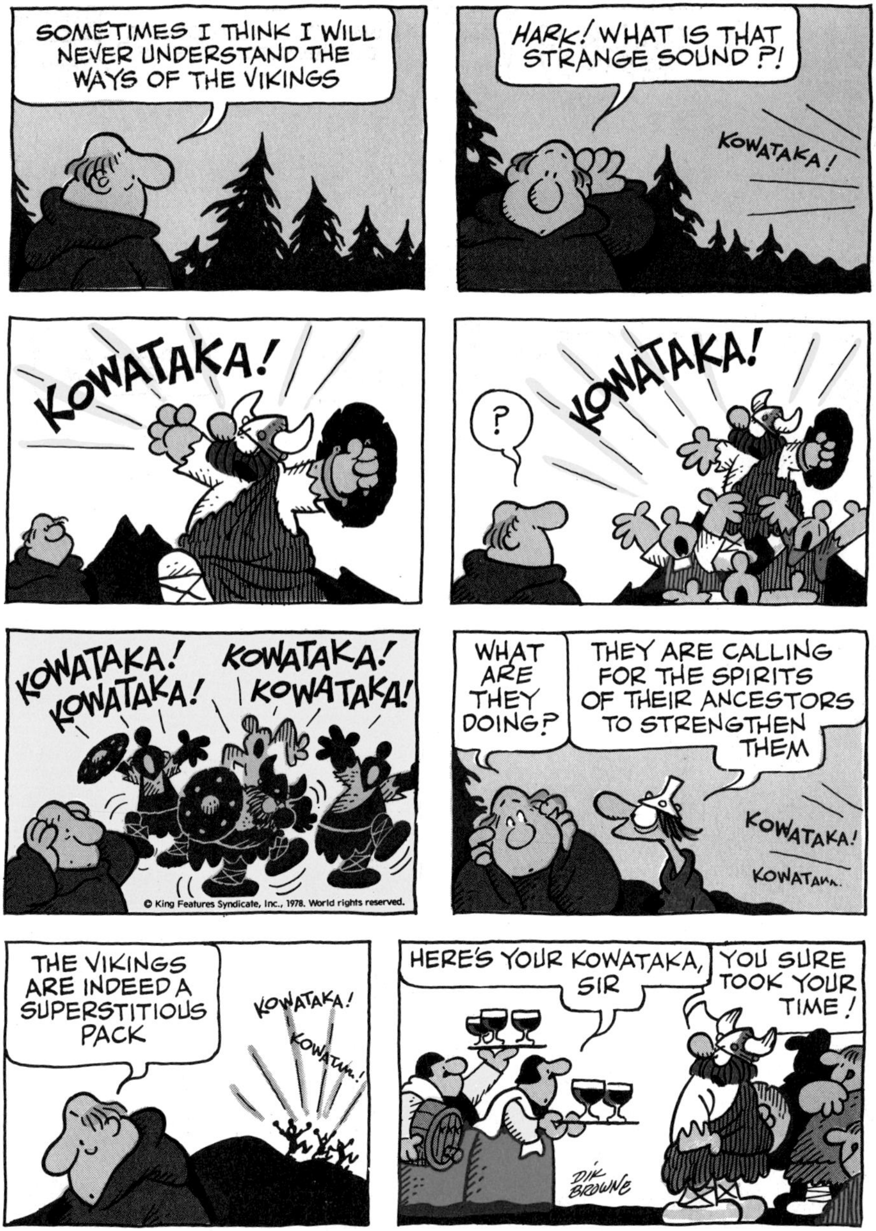
SOMETIMES I THINK I WILL NEVER UNDERSTAND THE WAYS OF THE VIKINGS
HARK! WHAT IS THAT STRANGE SOUND ?!
KOWATAKA!
KOWATAKA!
?
KOWATAKA!
KOWATAKA! KOWATAKA! KOWATAKA! KOWATAKA!
WHAT ARE THEY DOING?
THEY ARE CALLING FOR THE SPIRITS OF THEIR ANCESTORS TO STRENGTHEN THEM
KOWATAKA!
THE VIKINGS ARE INDEED A SUPERSTITIOUS PACK
KOWATAKA!
HERE'S YOUR KOWATAKA, SIR
YOU SURE TOOK YOUR TIME!
DIK BROWNE

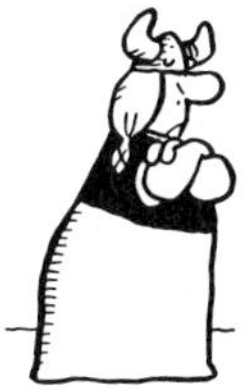

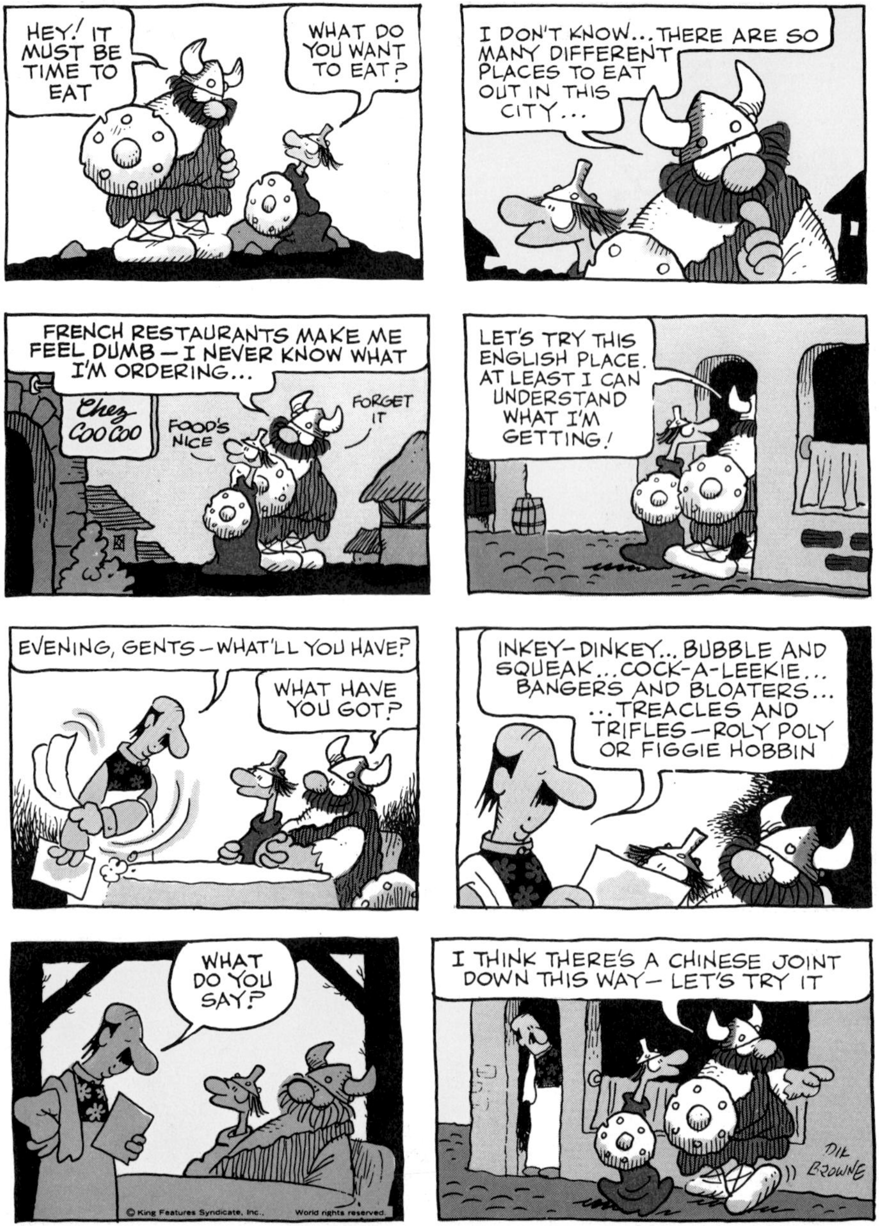
HEY! IT MUST BE TIME TO EAT
WHAT DO YOU WANT TO EAT?
I DON'T KNOW... THERE ARE SO MANY DIFFERENT PLACES TO EAT OUT IN THIS CITY...
FRENCH RESTAURANTS MAKE ME FEEL DUMB — I NEVER KNOW WHAT I'M ORDERING...
Chez CooCoo
FOOD'S NICE
FORGET IT
LET'S TRY THIS ENGLISH PLACE. AT LEAST I CAN UNDERSTAND WHAT I'M GETTING!
EVENING, GENTS — WHAT'LL YOU HAVE?
WHAT HAVE YOU GOT?
INKEY-DINKEY... BUBBLE AND SQUEAK... COCK-A-LEEKIE... BANGERS AND BLOATERS... ...TREACLES AND TRIFLES — ROLY POLY OR FIGGIE HOBBIN
WHAT DO YOU SAY?
© King Features Syndicate, Inc., World rights reserved.
I THINK THERE'S A CHINESE JOINT DOWN THIS WAY — LET'S TRY IT
DIK BROWNE

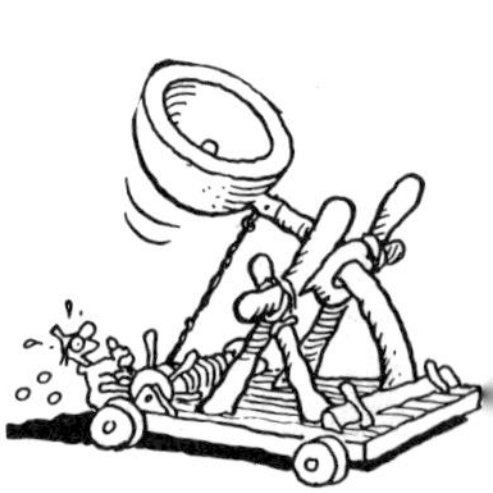

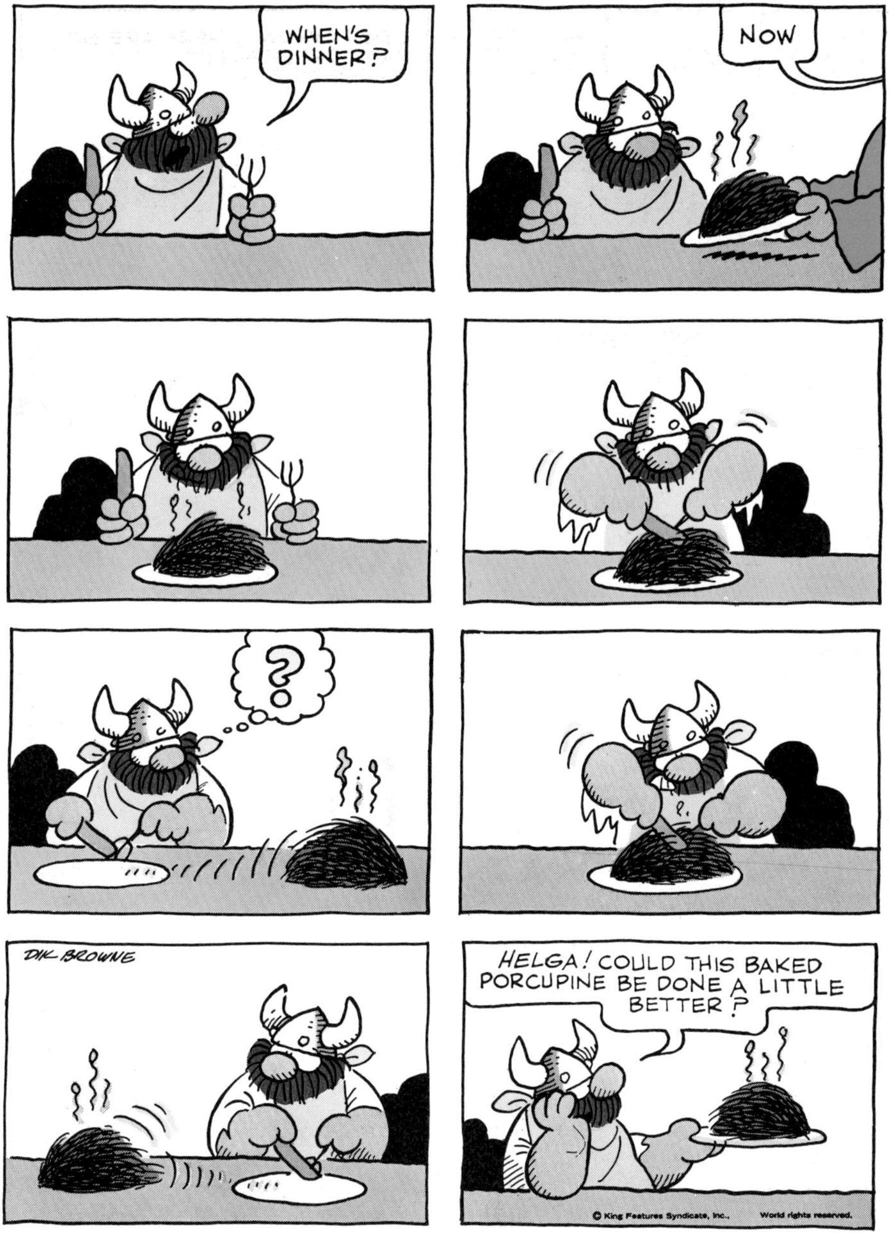
WHEN'S DINNER?
NOW
?
DIK BROWNE
HELGA! COULD THIS BAKED PORCUPINE BE DONE A LITTLE BETTER?
© King Features Syndicate, Inc., World rights reserved.

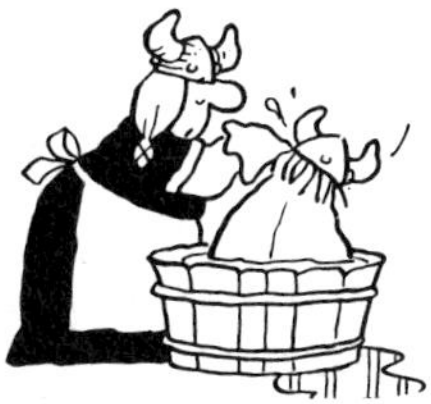

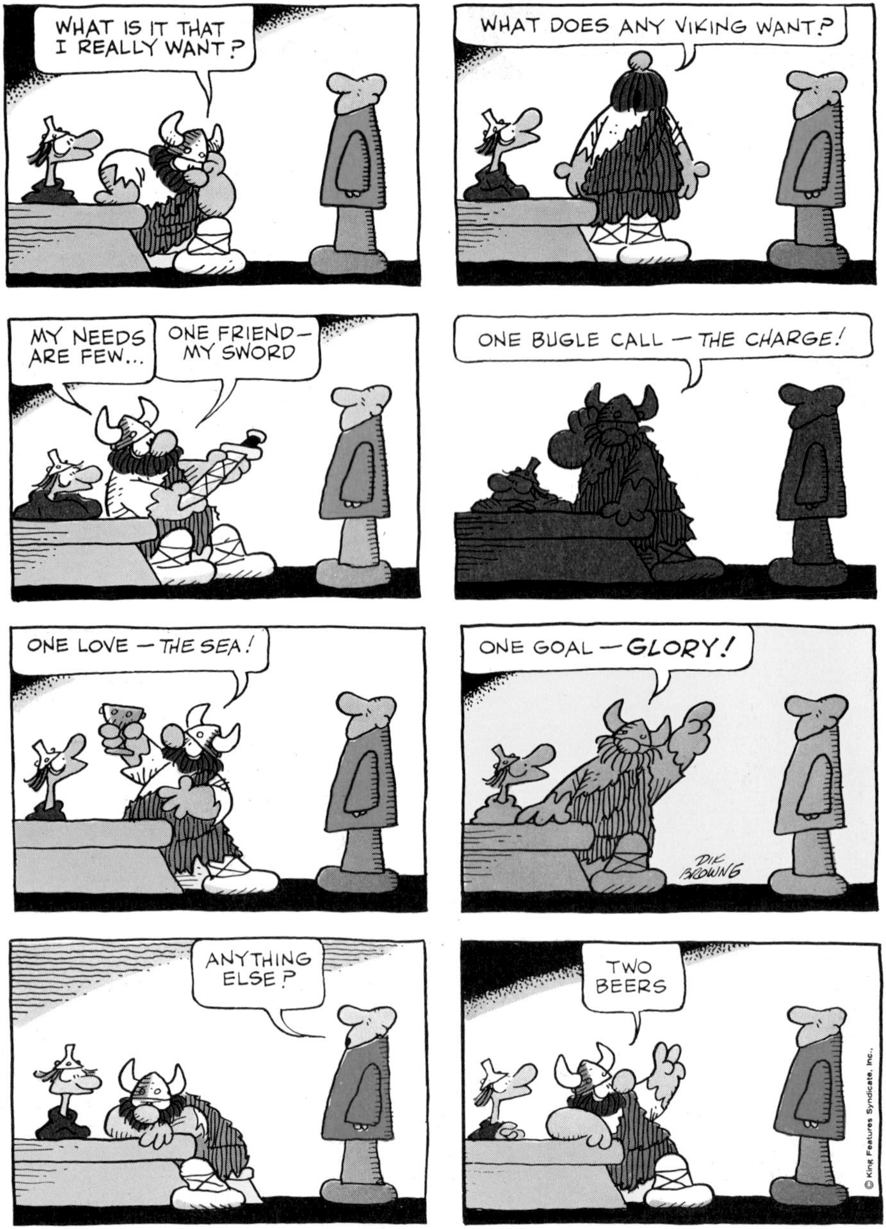
WHAT IS IT THAT I REALLY WANT?
WHAT DOES ANY VIKING WANT?
MY NEEDS ARE FEW...
ONE FRIEND— MY SWORD
ONE BUGLE CALL — THE CHARGE!
ONE LOVE — THE SEA!
ONE GOAL — GLORY!
DIK BROWNE
ANYTHING ELSE?
TWO BEERS
© King Features Syndicate, Inc.,

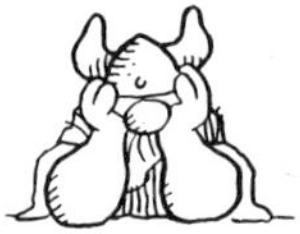

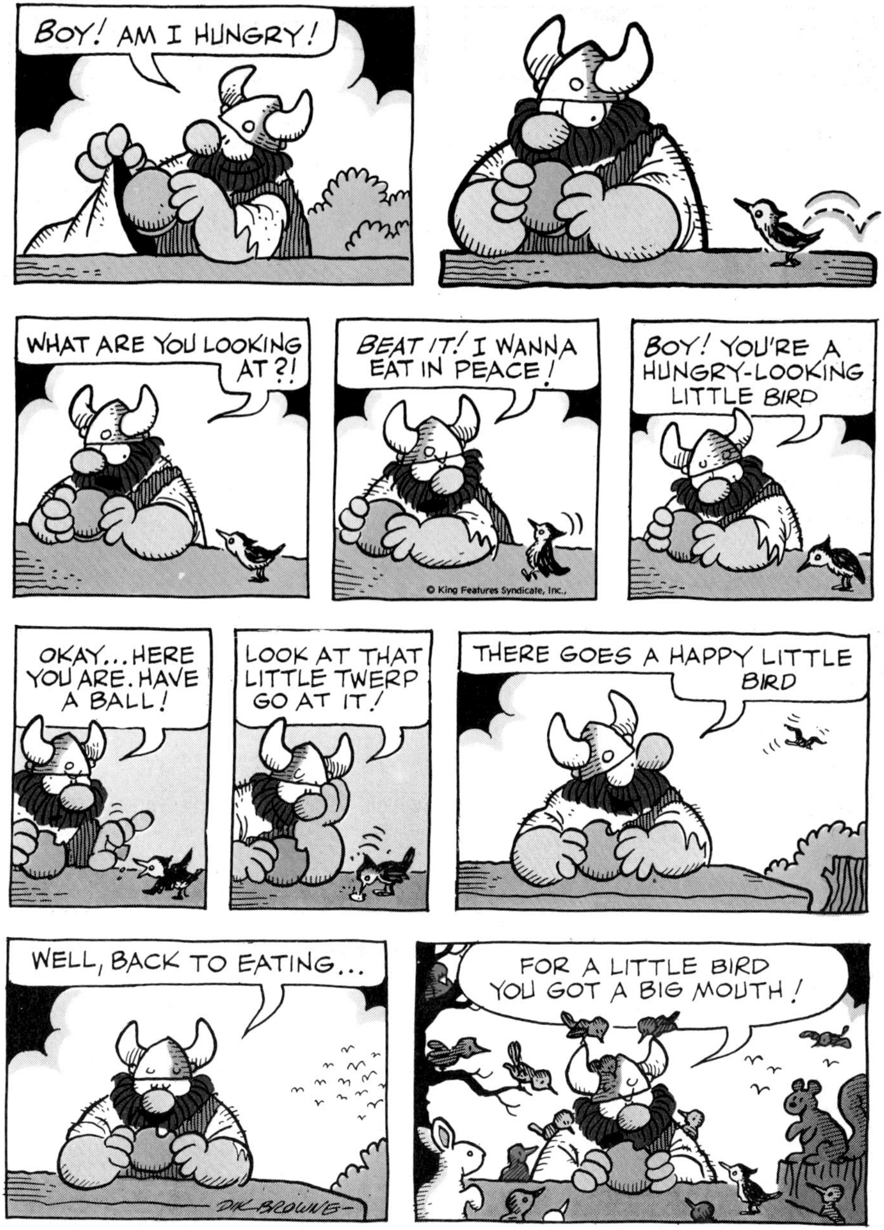
BOY! AM I HUNGRY!
WHAT ARE YOU LOOKING AT?!
BEAT IT! I WANNA EAT IN PEACE!
© King Features Syndicate, Inc.,
BOY! YOU'RE A HUNGRY-LOOKING LITTLE BIRD
OKAY... HERE YOU ARE. HAVE A BALL!
LOOK AT THAT LITTLE TWERP GO AT IT!
THERE GOES A HAPPY LITTLE BIRD
WELL, BACK TO EATING...
DIK BROWNE
FOR A LITTLE BIRD YOU GOT A BIG MOUTH!

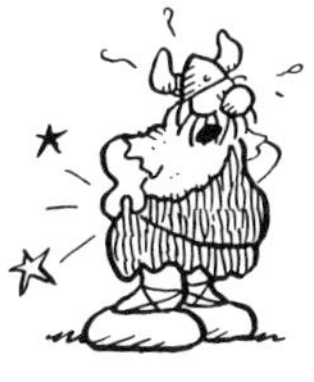

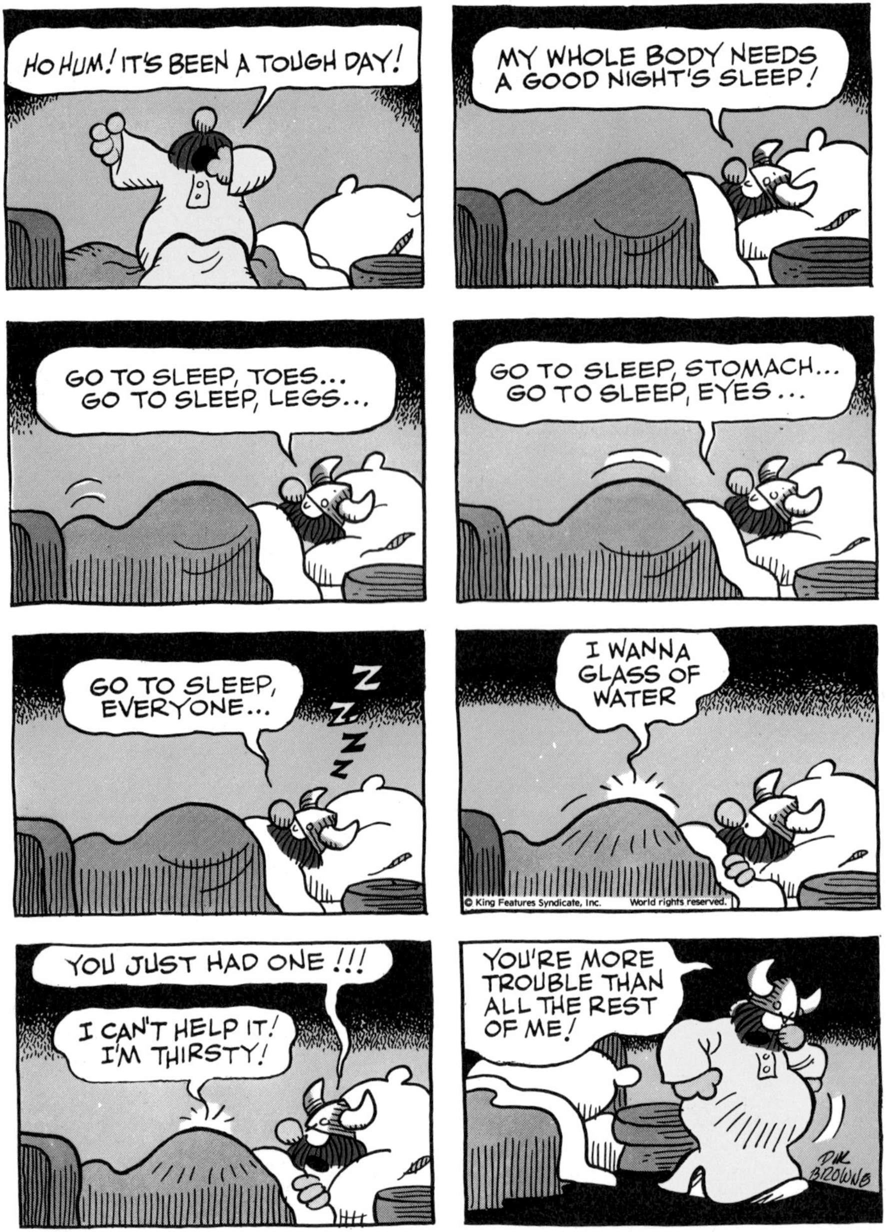
HO HUM! IT'S BEEN A TOUGH DAY!
MY WHOLE BODY NEEDS A GOOD NIGHT'S SLEEP!
GO TO SLEEP, TOES... GO TO SLEEP, LEGS...
GO TO SLEEP, STOMACH... GO TO SLEEP, EYES...
GO TO SLEEP, EVERYONE...
Z Z Z Z
I WANNA GLASS OF WATER
© King Features Syndicate, Inc. World rights reserved.
YOU JUST HAD ONE!!!
I CAN'T HELP IT! I'M THIRSTY!
YOU'RE MORE TROUBLE THAN ALL THE REST OF ME!
DIK BROWNE

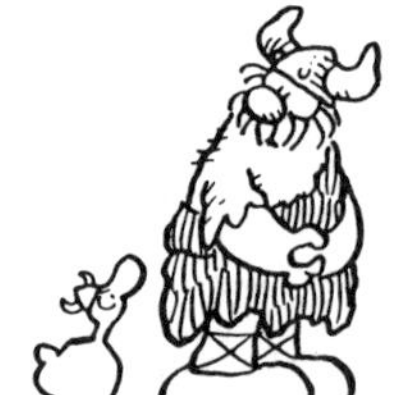

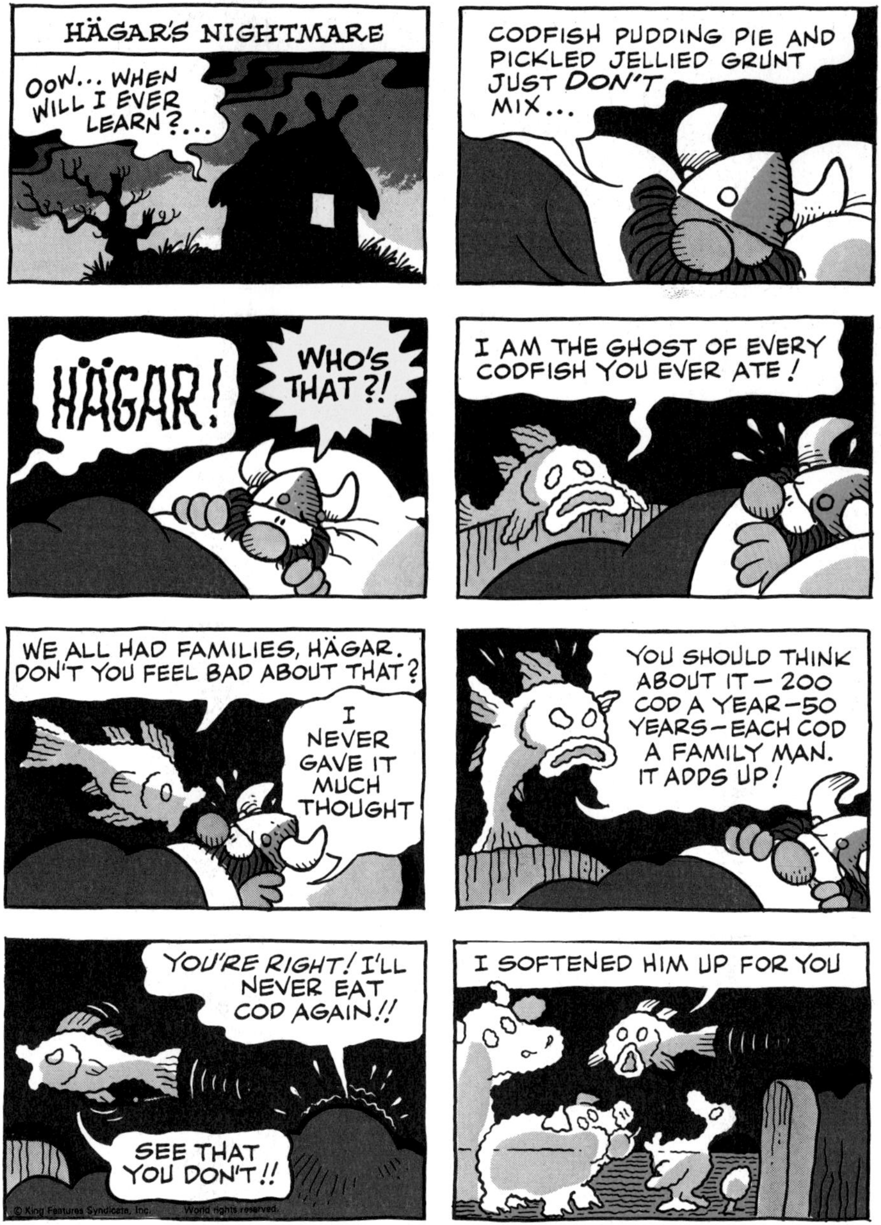
HÄGAR'S NIGHTMARE
OOW... WHEN WILL I EVER LEARN?...
CODFISH PUDDING PIE AND PICKLED JELLIED GRUNT JUST DON'T MIX...
HÄGAR!
WHO'S THAT?!
I AM THE GHOST OF EVERY CODFISH YOU EVER ATE!
WE ALL HAD FAMILIES, HÄGAR. DON'T YOU FEEL BAD ABOUT THAT?
I NEVER GAVE IT MUCH THOUGHT
YOU SHOULD THINK ABOUT IT — 200 COD A YEAR—50 YEARS—EACH COD A FAMILY MAN. IT ADDS UP!
YOU'RE RIGHT! I'LL NEVER EAT COD AGAIN!!
SEE THAT YOU DON'T!!
© King Features Syndicate, Inc. World rights reserved.
I SOFTENED HIM UP FOR YOU

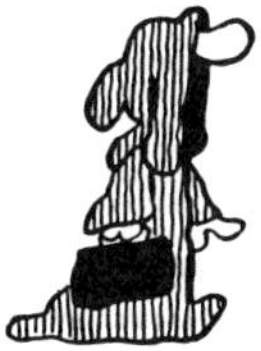

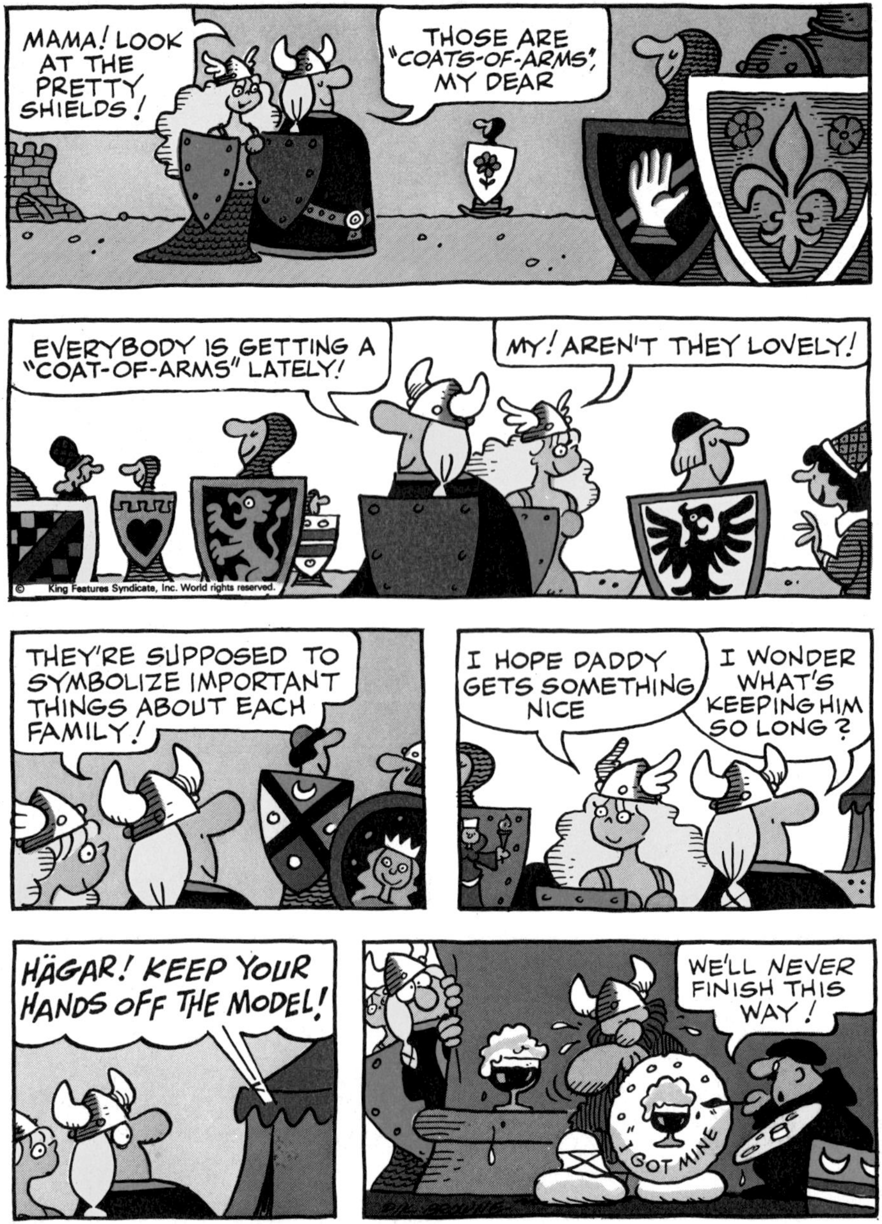
MAMA! LOOK AT THE PRETTY SHIELDS!
THOSE ARE "COATS-OF-ARMS", MY DEAR
EVERYBODY IS GETTING A "COAT-OF-ARMS" LATELY!
MY! AREN'T THEY LOVELY!
© King Features Syndicate, Inc. World rights reserved.
THEY'RE SUPPOSED TO SYMBOLIZE IMPORTANT THINGS ABOUT EACH FAMILY!
I HOPE DADDY GETS SOMETHING NICE
I WONDER WHAT'S KEEPING HIM SO LONG?
HÄGAR! KEEP YOUR HANDS OFF THE MODEL!
WE'LL NEVER FINISH THIS WAY!
"I GOT MINE"

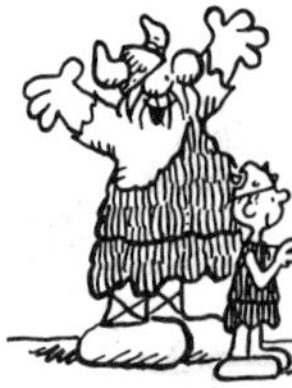

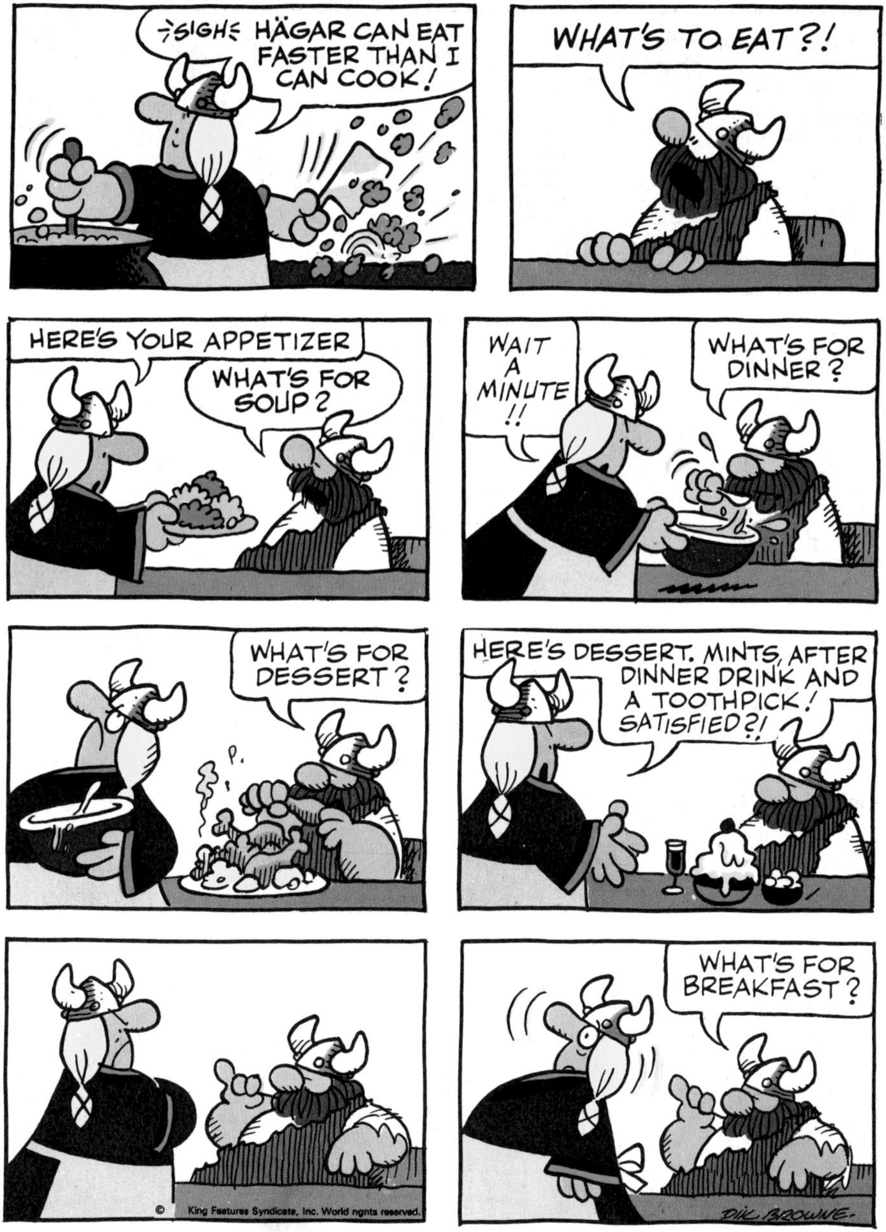

-SIGH- HÄGAR CAN EAT FASTER THAN I CAN COOK!
WHAT'S TO EAT?!
HERE'S YOUR APPETIZER
WHAT'S FOR SOUP?
WAIT A MINUTE!!
WHAT'S FOR DINNER?
WHAT'S FOR DESSERT?
HERE'S DESSERT. MINTS, AFTER DINNER DRINK AND A TOOTHPICK! SATISFIED?!
WHAT'S FOR BREAKFAST?
© King Features Syndicate, Inc. World rights reserved.
DIK BROWNE

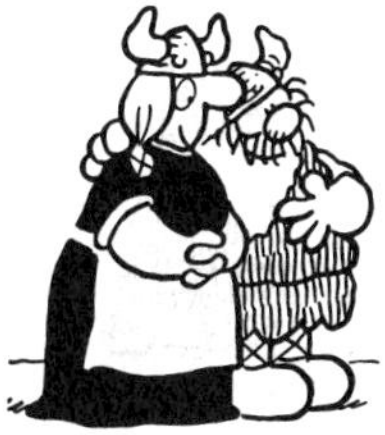

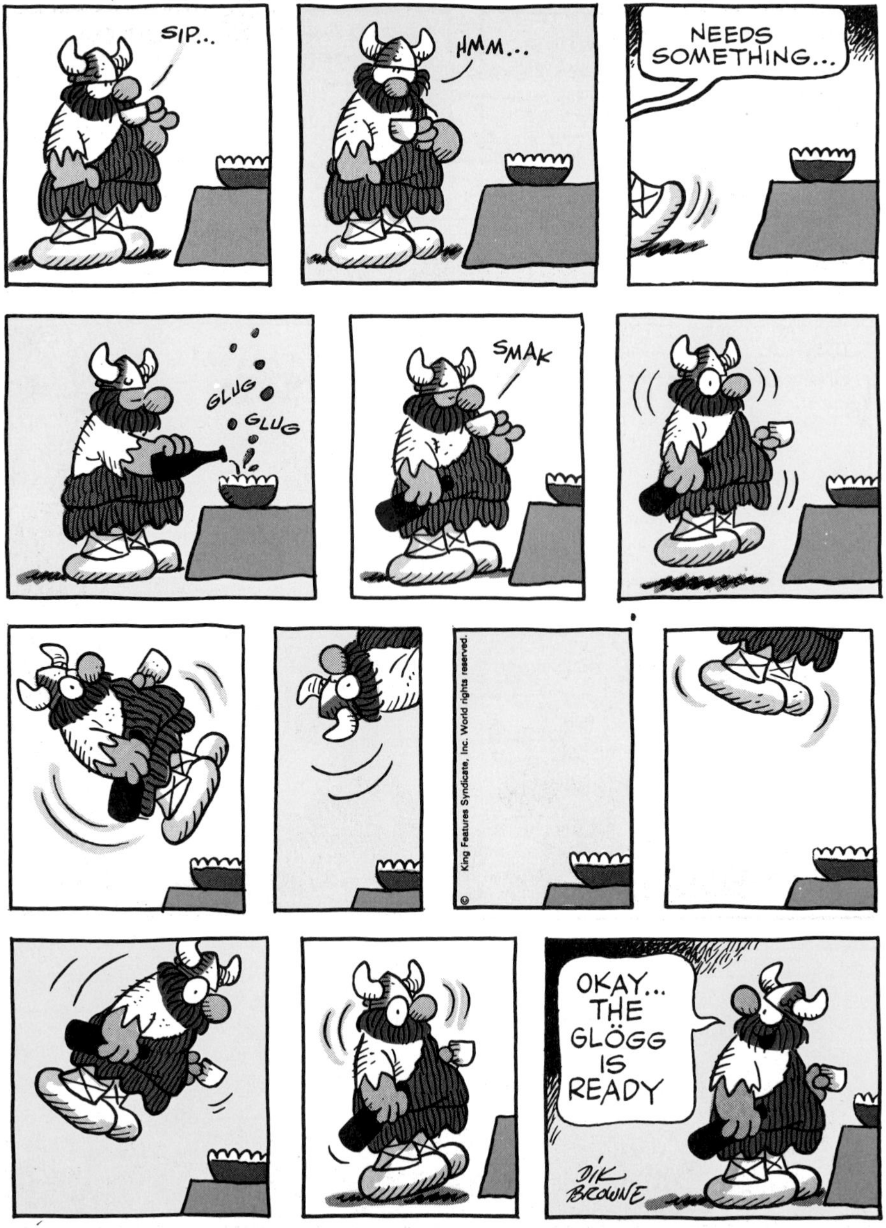
SIP...
HMM...
NEEDS SOMETHING...
GLUG
GLUG
SMAK
© King Features Syndicate, Inc. World rights reserved.
OKAY... THE GLÖGG IS READY
DIK BROWNE

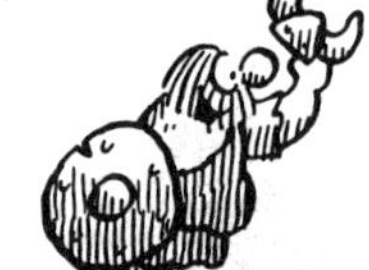

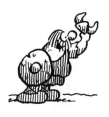

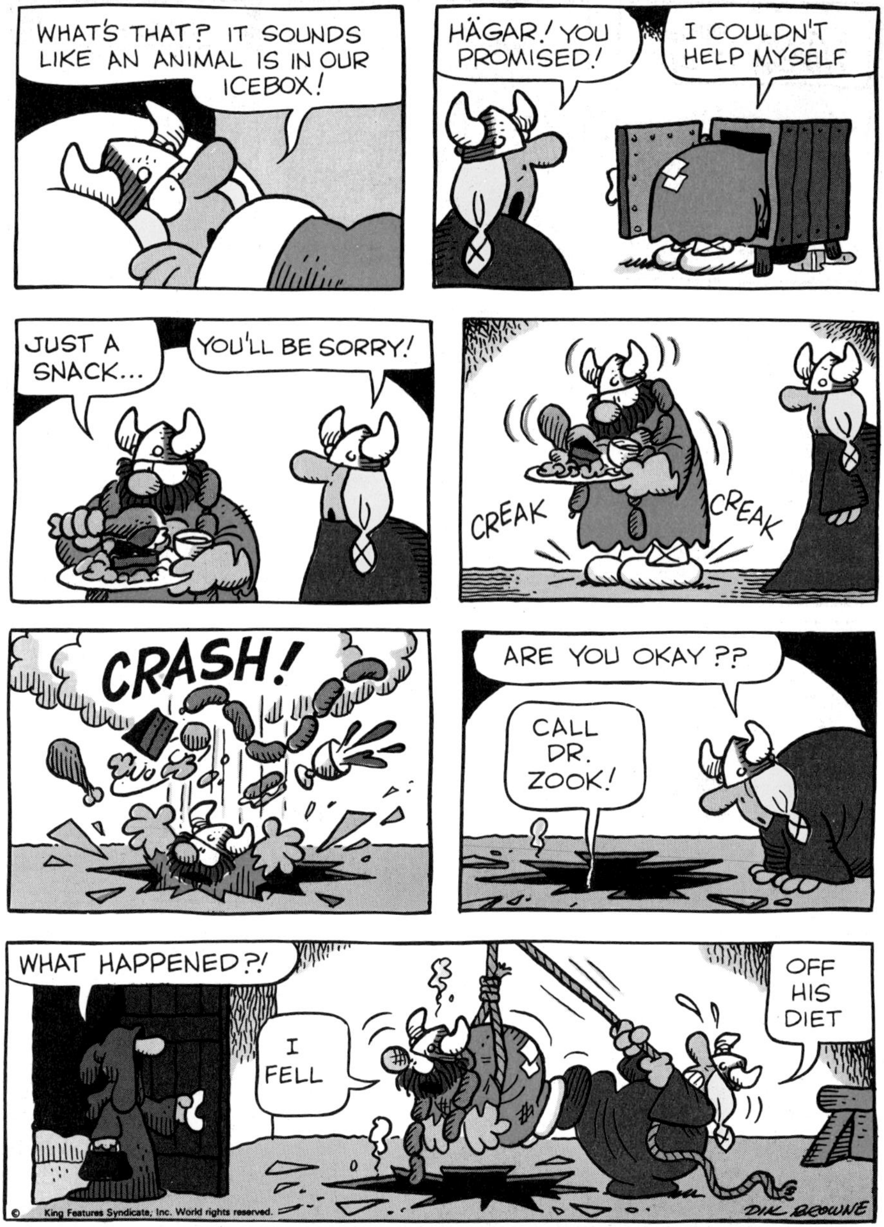
WHAT'S THAT? IT SOUNDS LIKE AN ANIMAL IS IN OUR ICEBOX!
HÄGAR! YOU PROMISED!
I COULDN'T HELP MYSELF
JUST A SNACK...
YOU'LL BE SORRY!
CREAK
CREAK
CRASH!
ARE YOU OKAY??
CALL DR. ZOOK!
WHAT HAPPENED?!
I FELL
OFF HIS DIET
DIK BROWNE

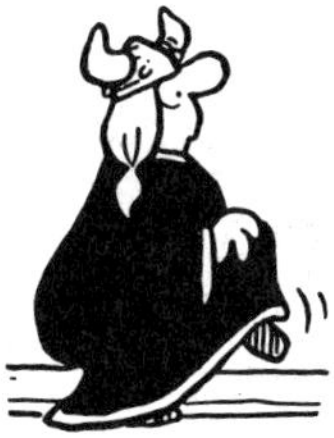

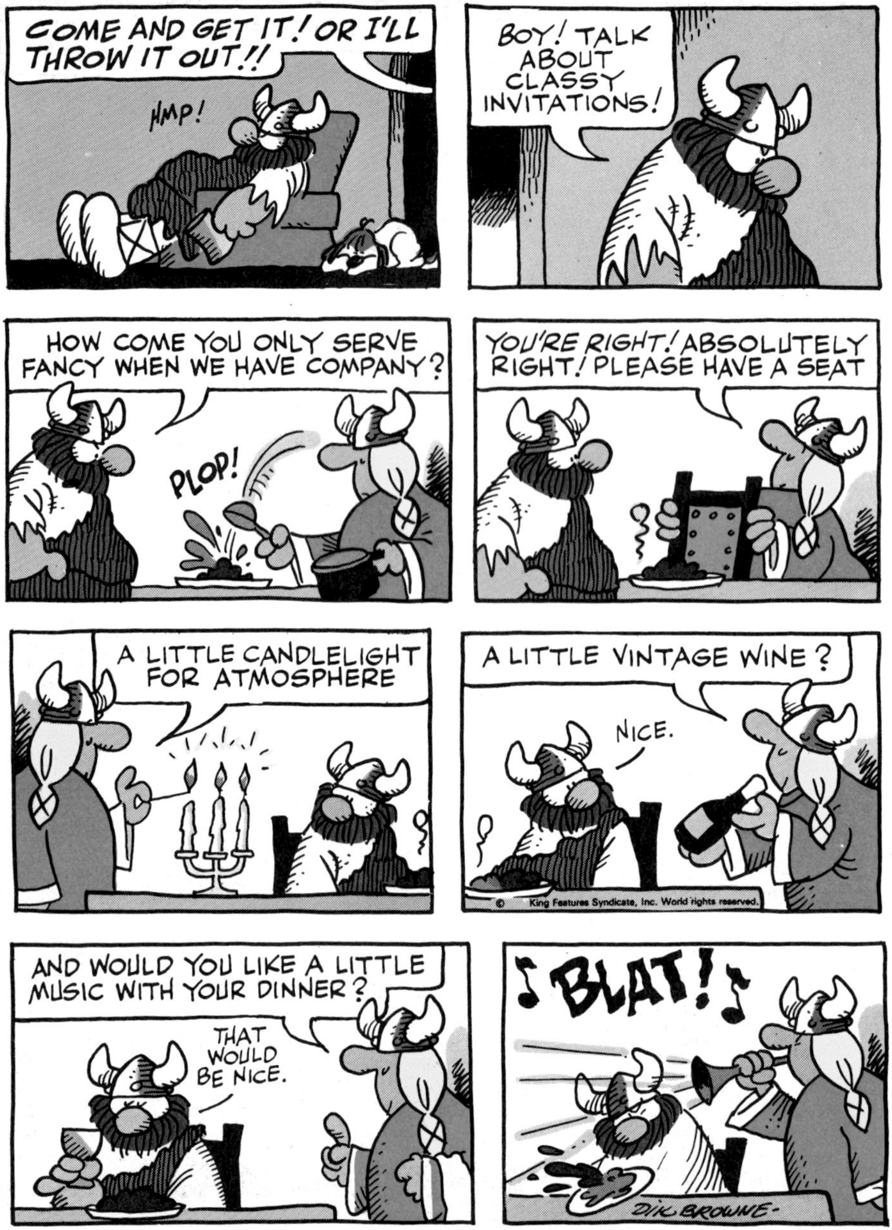
COME AND GET IT! OR I'LL THROW IT OUT!!
HMP!
BOY! TALK ABOUT CLASSY INVITATIONS!
HOW COME YOU ONLY SERVE FANCY WHEN WE HAVE COMPANY?
PLOP!
YOU'RE RIGHT! ABSOLUTELY RIGHT! PLEASE HAVE A SEAT
A LITTLE CANDLELIGHT FOR ATMOSPHERE
A LITTLE VINTAGE WINE?
NICE.
© King Features Syndicate, Inc. World rights reserved.
AND WOULD YOU LIKE A LITTLE MUSIC WITH YOUR DINNER?
THAT WOULD BE NICE.
BLAT!
DIK BROWNE

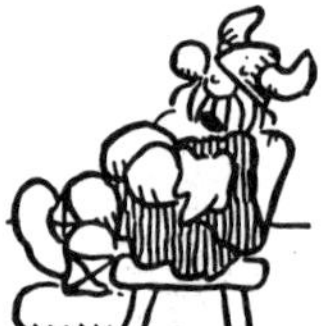

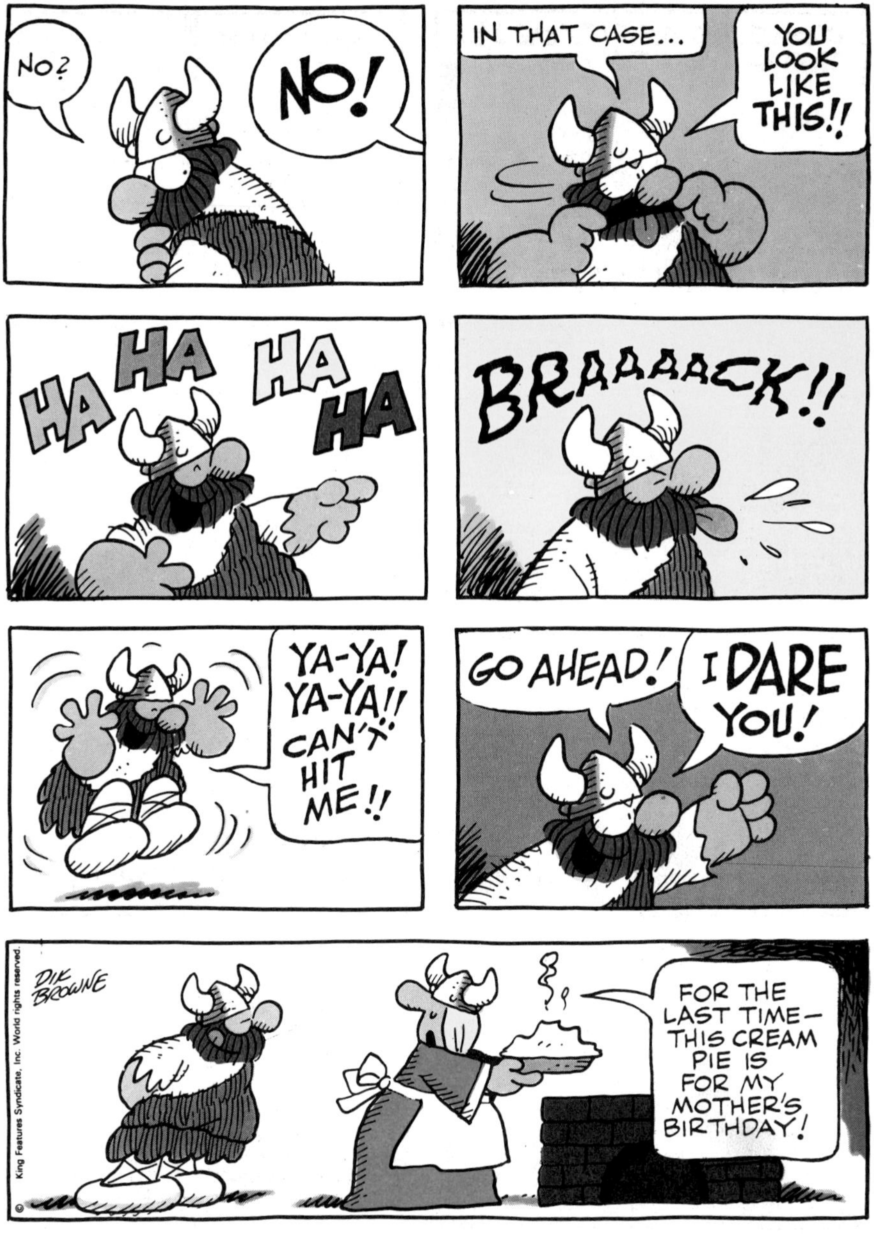
NO?
NO!
IN THAT CASE...
YOU LOOK LIKE THIS!!
HA HA HA HA
BRAAAACK!!
YA-YA! YA-YA!! CAN'T HIT ME!!
GO AHEAD!
I DARE YOU!
© King Features Syndicate, Inc. World rights reserved.
DIK BROWNE
FOR THE LAST TIME— THIS CREAM PIE IS FOR MY MOTHER'S BIRTHDAY!

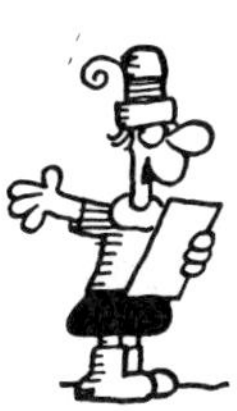

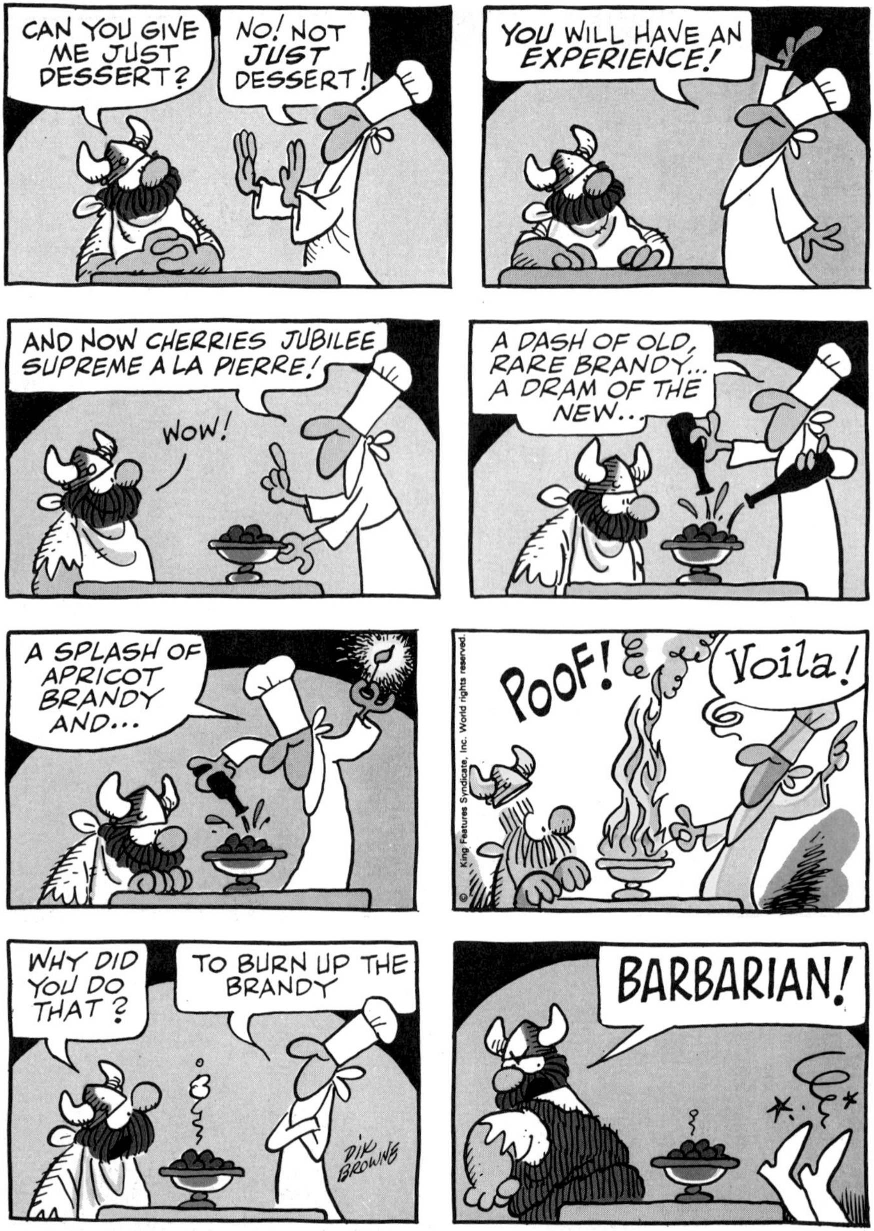
CAN YOU GIVE ME JUST DESSERT?
NO! NOT JUST DESSERT!
YOU WILL HAVE AN EXPERIENCE!
AND NOW CHERRIES JUBILEE SUPREME A LA PIERRE!
WOW!
A DASH OF OLD, RARE BRANDY... A DRAM OF THE NEW...
A SPLASH OF APRICOT BRANDY AND...
© King Features Syndicate, Inc. World rights reserved.
POOF!
Voila!
WHY DID YOU DO THAT?
TO BURN UP THE BRANDY
DIK BROWNE
BARBARIAN!

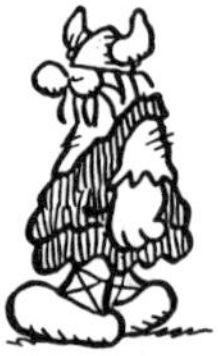

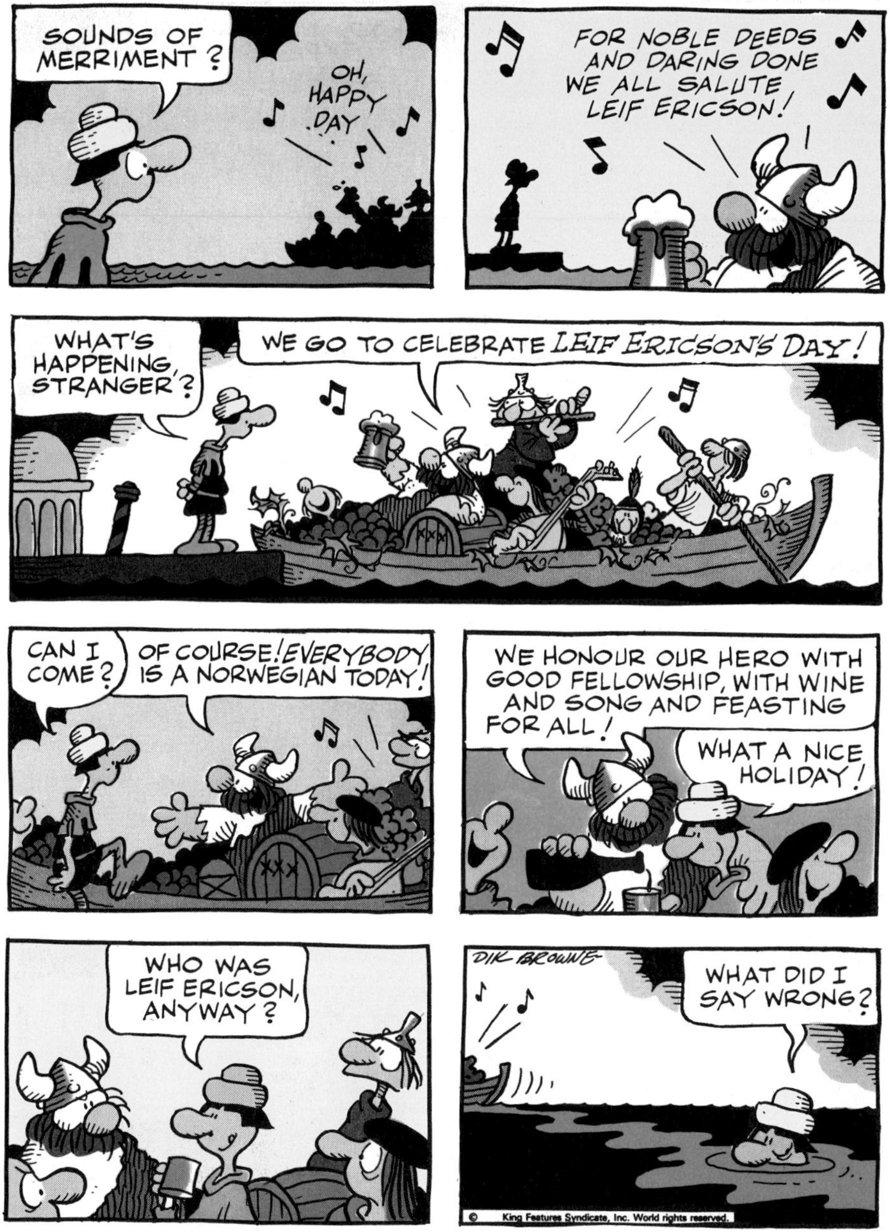
SOUNDS OF MERRIMENT?
OH, HAPPY DAY
FOR NOBLE DEEDS AND DARING DONE WE ALL SALUTE LEIF ERICSON!
WHAT'S HAPPENING, STRANGER?
WE GO TO CELEBRATE LEIF ERICSON'S DAY!
CAN I COME?
OF COURSE! EVERYBODY IS A NORWEGIAN TODAY!
WE HONOUR OUR HERO WITH GOOD FELLOWSHIP, WITH WINE AND SONG AND FEASTING FOR ALL!
WHAT A NICE HOLIDAY!
WHO WAS LEIF ERICSON, ANYWAY?
DIK BROWNE
WHAT DID I SAY WRONG?
© King Features Syndicate, Inc. World rights reserved.

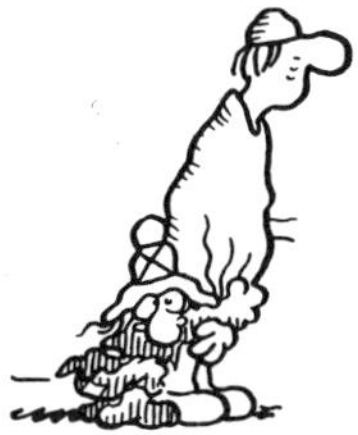

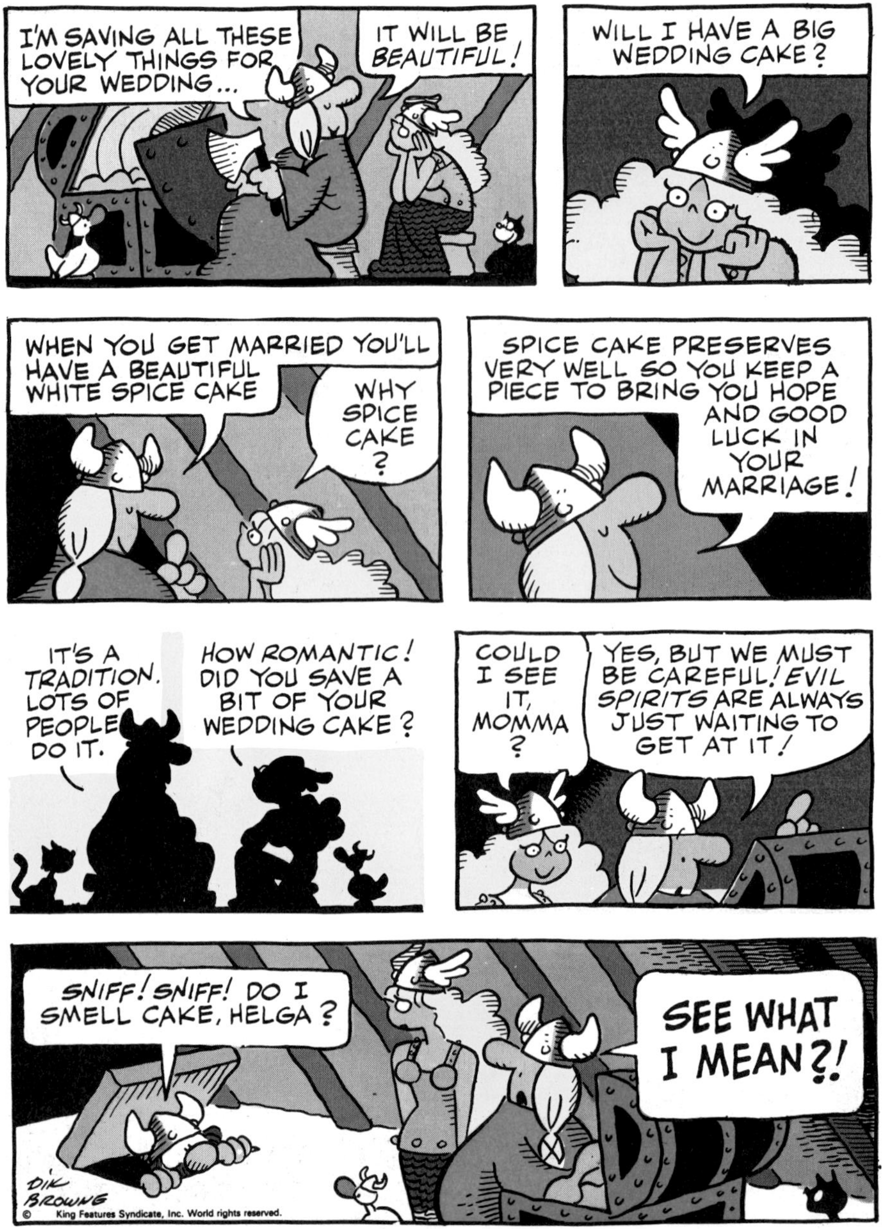
I'M SAVING ALL THESE LOVELY THINGS FOR YOUR WEDDING...
IT WILL BE BEAUTIFUL!
WILL I HAVE A BIG WEDDING CAKE?
WHEN YOU GET MARRIED YOU'LL HAVE A BEAUTIFUL WHITE SPICE CAKE
WHY SPICE CAKE?
SPICE CAKE PRESERVES VERY WELL SO YOU KEEP A PIECE TO BRING YOU HOPE AND GOOD LUCK IN YOUR MARRIAGE!
IT'S A TRADITION. LOTS OF PEOPLE DO IT.
HOW ROMANTIC! DID YOU SAVE A BIT OF YOUR WEDDING CAKE?
COULD I SEE IT, MOMMA?
YES, BUT WE MUST BE CAREFUL! EVIL SPIRITS ARE ALWAYS JUST WAITING TO GET AT IT!
SNIFF! SNIFF! DO I SMELL CAKE, HELGA?
SEE WHAT I MEAN?!
DIK BROWNE
© King Features Syndicate, Inc. World rights reserved.

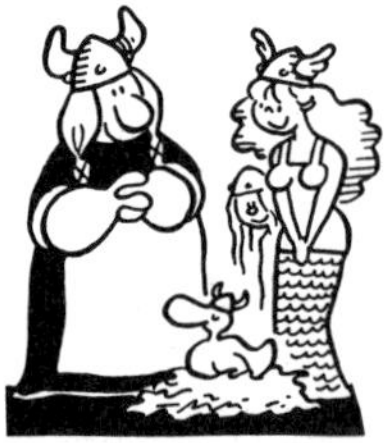

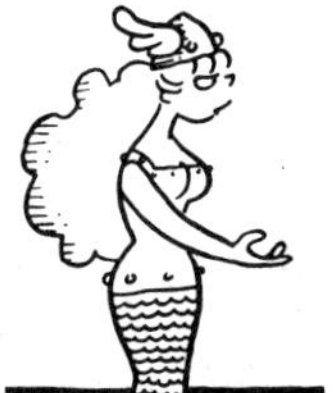

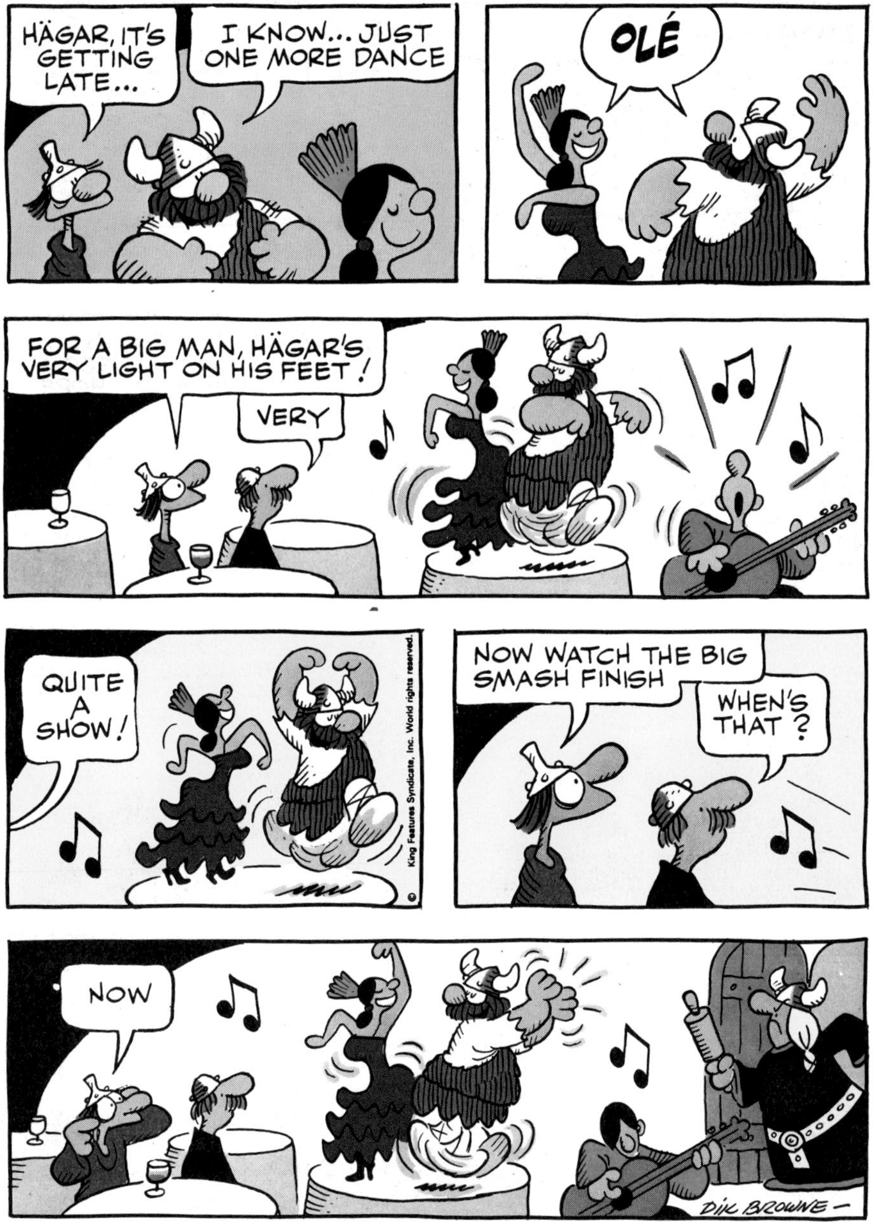
HÄGAR, IT'S GETTING LATE...
I KNOW... JUST ONE MORE DANCE
OLÉ
FOR A BIG MAN, HÄGAR'S VERY LIGHT ON HIS FEET!
VERY
QUITE A SHOW!
© King Features Syndicate, Inc. World rights reserved.
NOW WATCH THE BIG SMASH FINISH
WHEN'S THAT?
NOW
DIK BROWNE

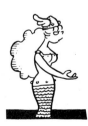

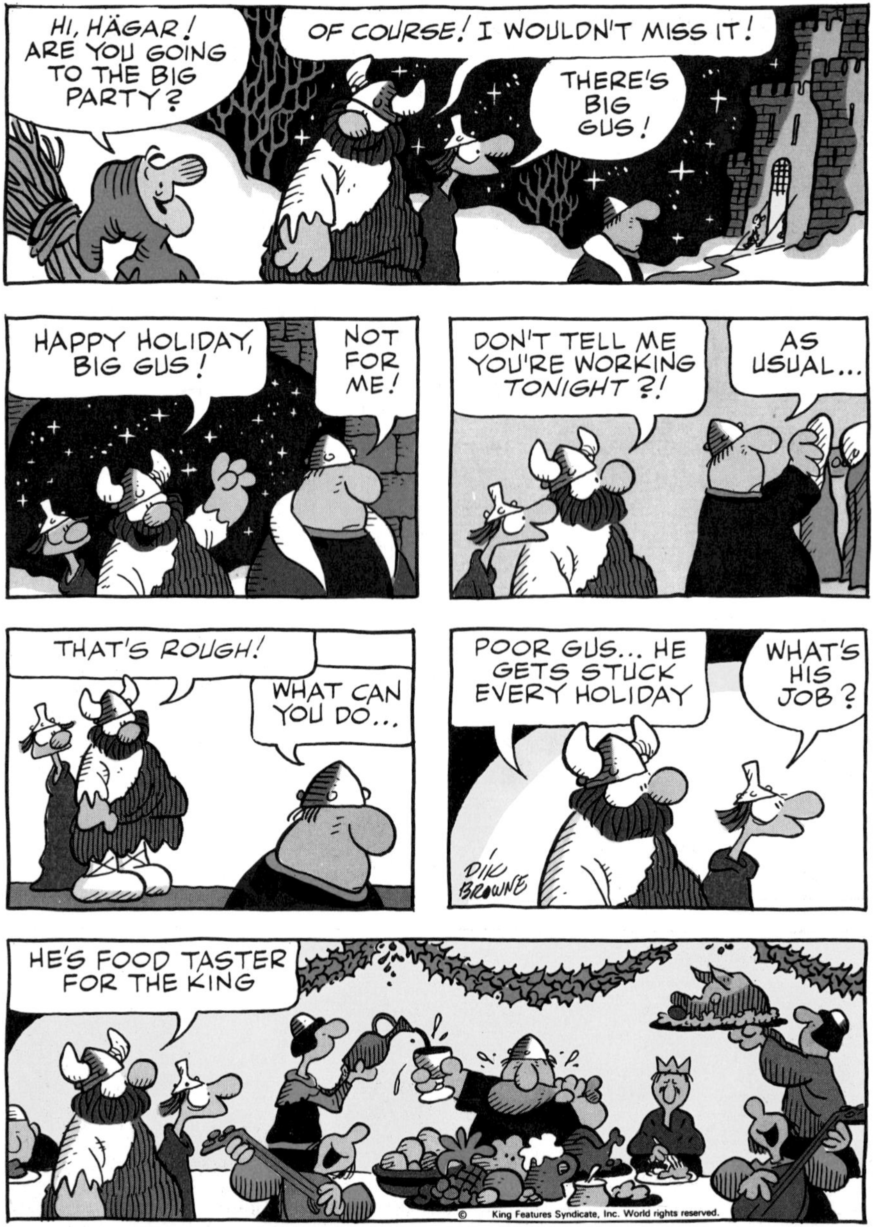
HI, HÄGAR! ARE YOU GOING TO THE BIG PARTY?
OF COURSE! I WOULDN'T MISS IT!
THERE'S BIG GUS!
HAPPY HOLIDAY, BIG GUS!
NOT FOR ME!
DON'T TELL ME YOU'RE WORKING TONIGHT?!
AS USUAL...
THAT'S ROUGH!
WHAT CAN YOU DO...
POOR GUS... HE GETS STUCK EVERY HOLIDAY
WHAT'S HIS JOB?
DIK BROWNE
HE'S FOOD TASTER FOR THE KING
© King Features Syndicate, Inc. World rights reserved.

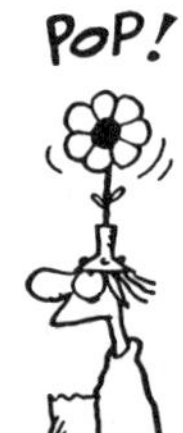
POP!

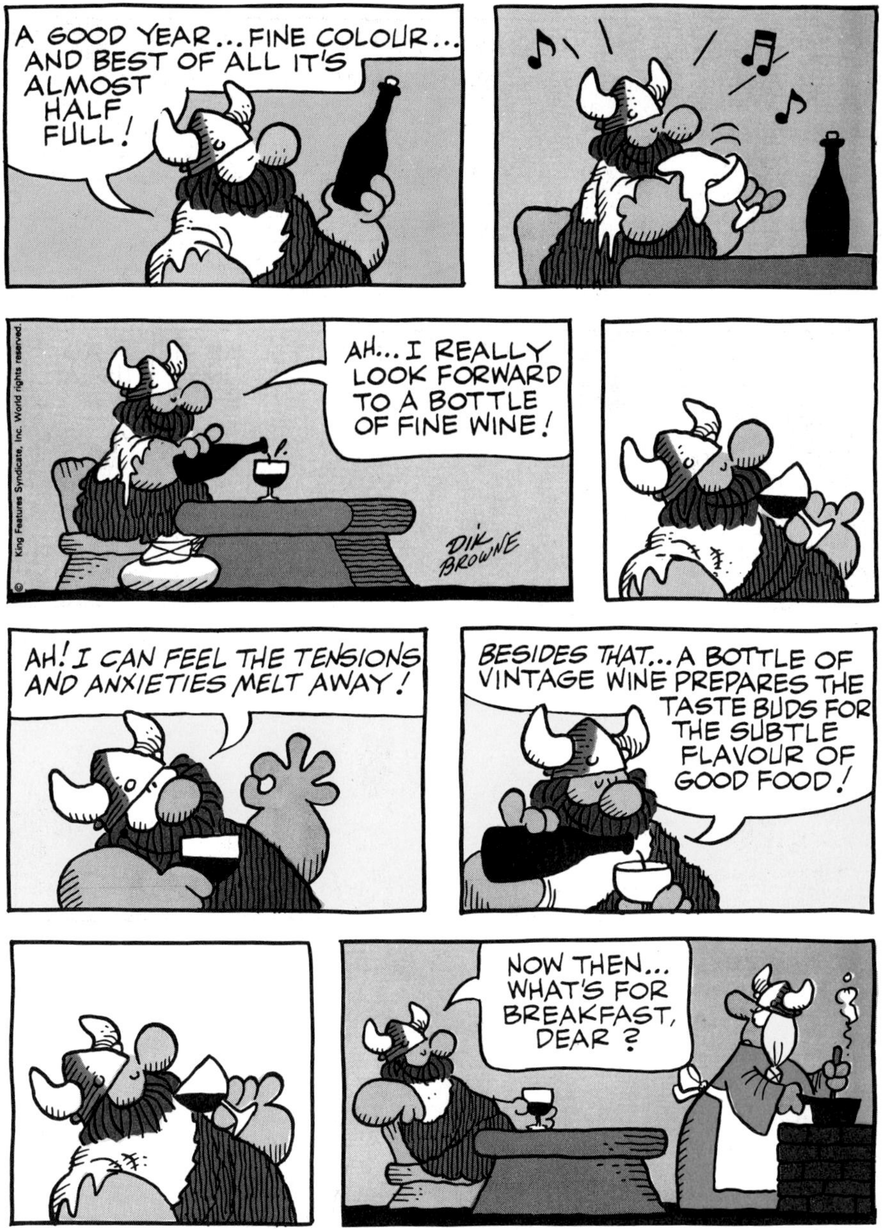
A GOOD YEAR... FINE COLOUR... AND BEST OF ALL IT'S ALMOST HALF FULL!
AH... I REALLY LOOK FORWARD TO A BOTTLE OF FINE WINE!
© King Features Syndicate, Inc. World rights reserved.
DIK BROWNE
AH! I CAN FEEL THE TENSIONS AND ANXIETIES MELT AWAY!
BESIDES THAT... A BOTTLE OF VINTAGE WINE PREPARES THE TASTE BUDS FOR THE SUBTLE FLAVOUR OF GOOD FOOD!
NOW THEN... WHAT'S FOR BREAKFAST, DEAR?

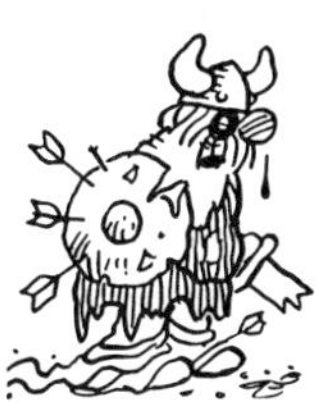

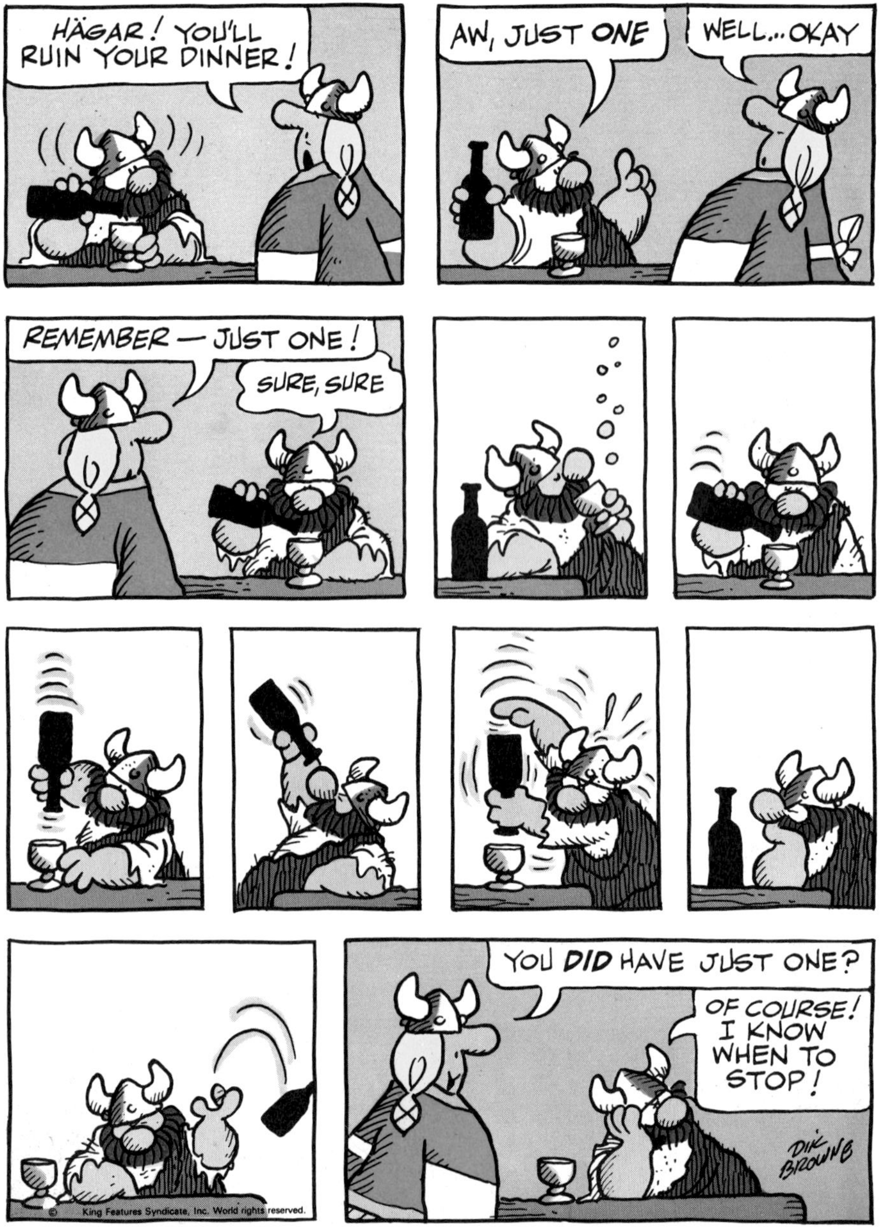
HÄGAR! YOU'LL RUIN YOUR DINNER!
AW, JUST ONE
WELL... OKAY
REMEMBER — JUST ONE!
SURE, SURE
YOU DID HAVE JUST ONE?
OF COURSE! I KNOW WHEN TO STOP!
DIK BROWNE
© King Features Syndicate, Inc. World rights reserved.

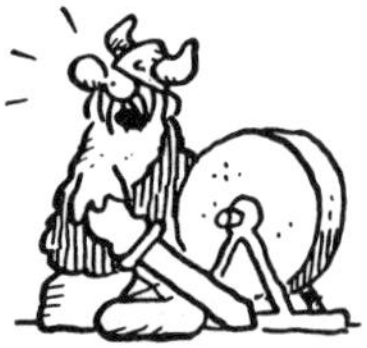

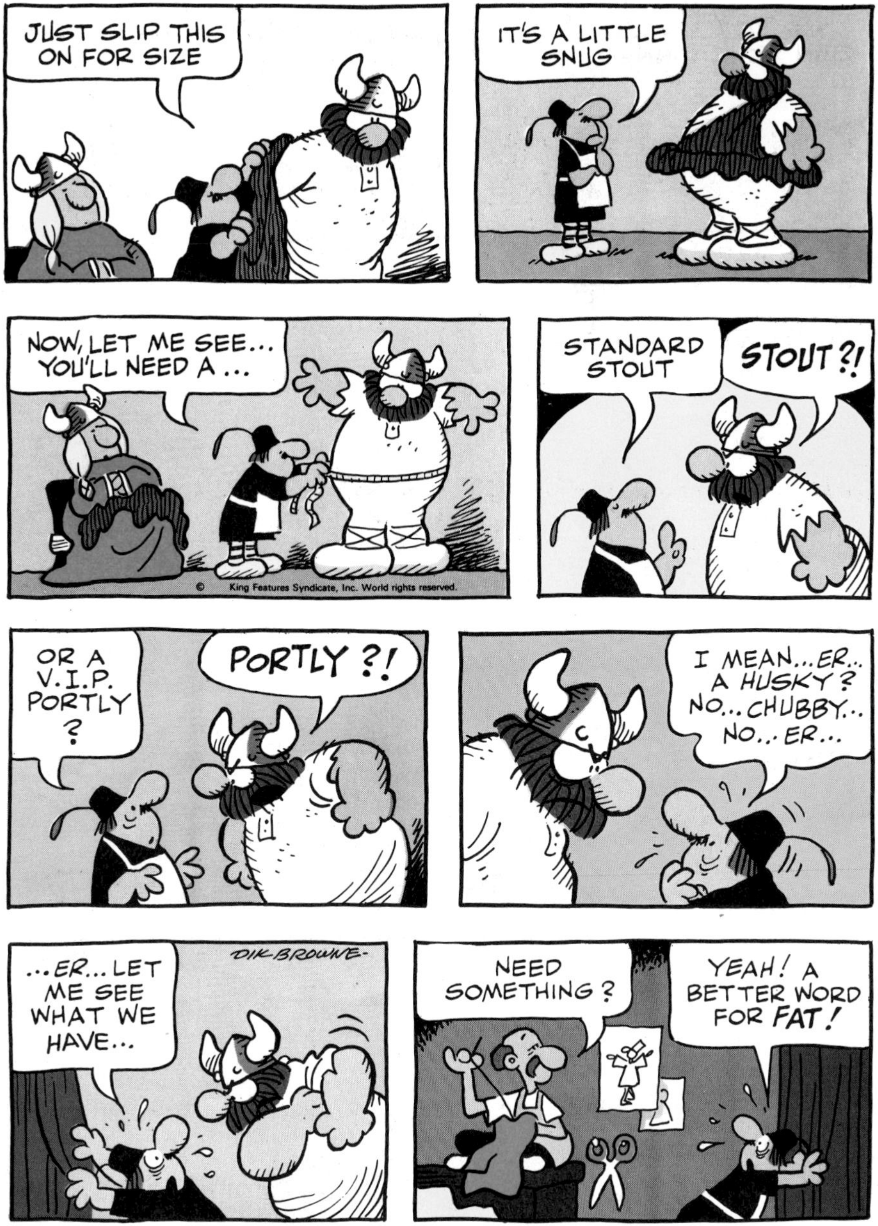
JUST SLIP THIS ON FOR SIZE
IT'S A LITTLE SNUG
NOW, LET ME SEE... YOU'LL NEED A ...
© King Features Syndicate, Inc. World rights reserved.
STANDARD STOUT
STOUT ?!
OR A V.I.P. PORTLY ?
PORTLY ?!
I MEAN...ER... A HUSKY ? NO...CHUBBY... NO... ER...
DIK BROWNE
...ER... LET ME SEE WHAT WE HAVE...
NEED SOMETHING ?
YEAH! A BETTER WORD FOR FAT!

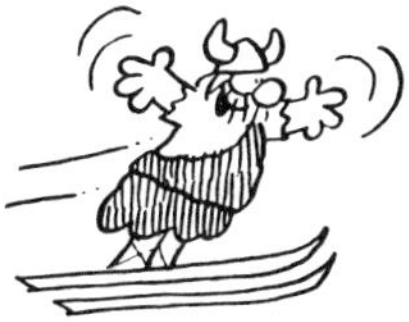

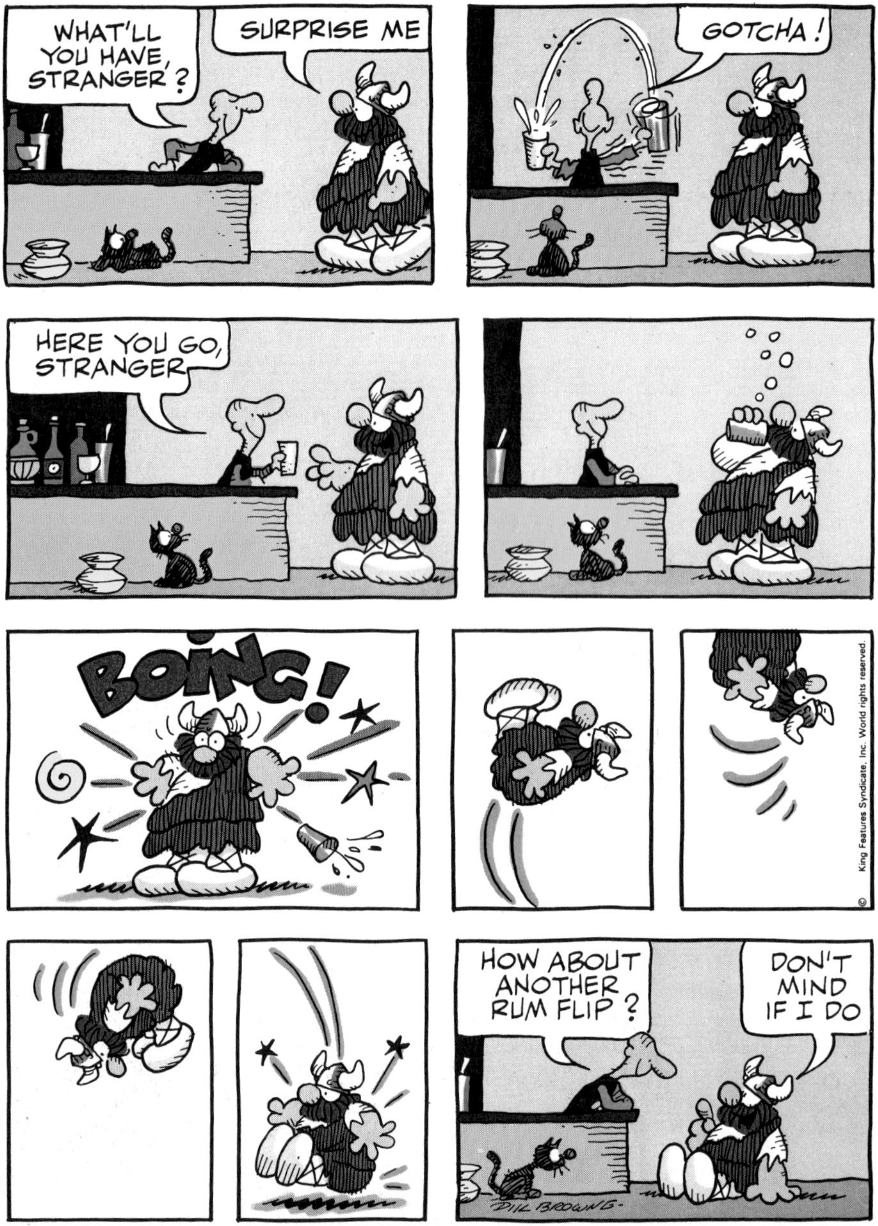
WHAT'LL YOU HAVE, STRANGER ?
SURPRISE ME
GOTCHA !
HERE YOU GO, STRANGER
BOING!
© King Features Syndicate, Inc. World rights reserved.
HOW ABOUT ANOTHER RUM FLIP ?
DON'T MIND IF I DO

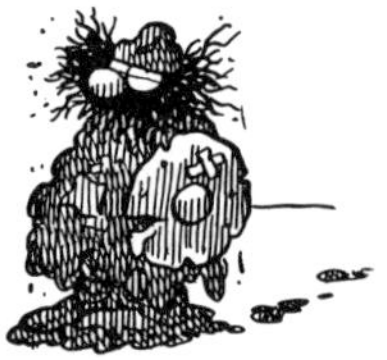

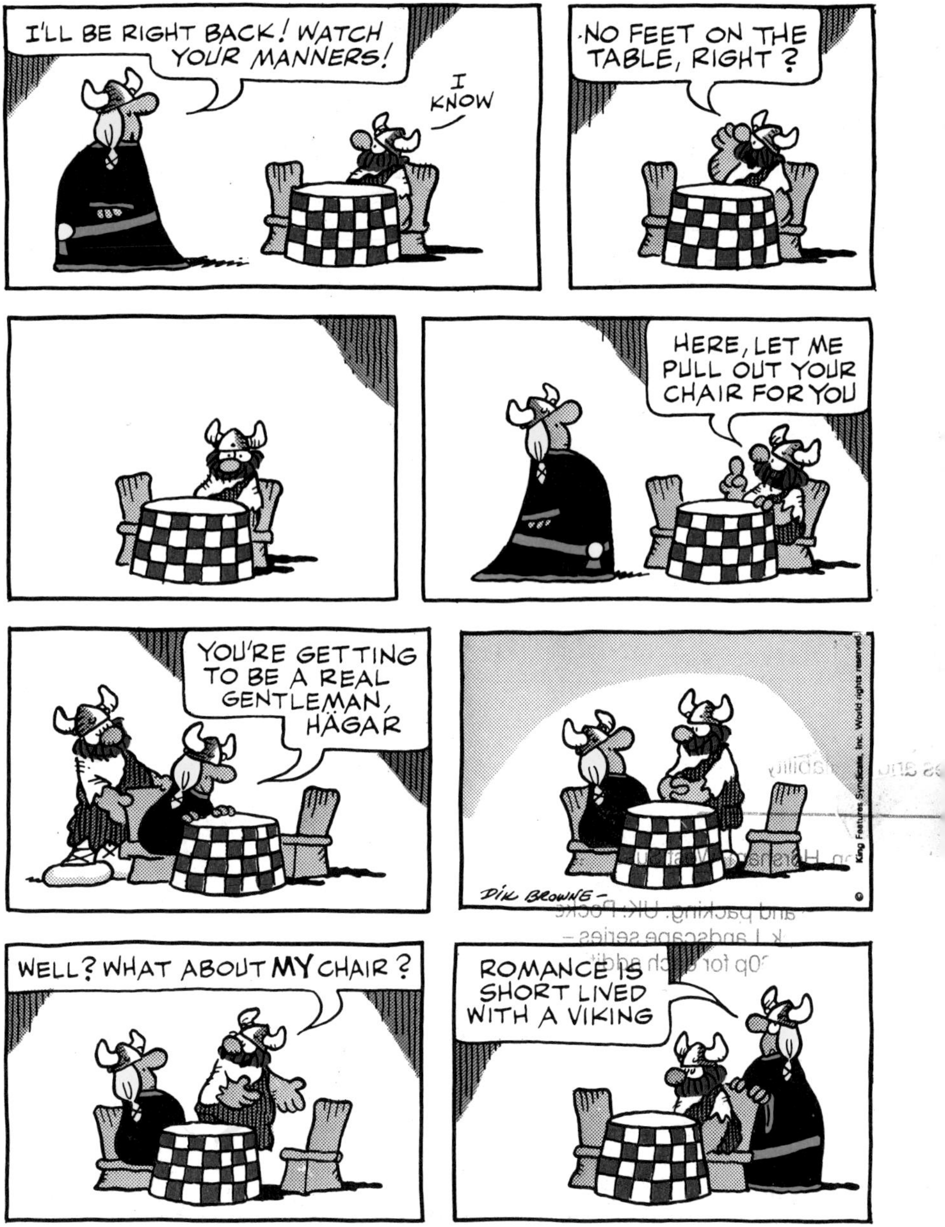
I'LL BE RIGHT BACK! WATCH YOUR MANNERS!
I KNOW
NO FEET ON THE TABLE, RIGHT?
HERE, LET ME PULL OUT YOUR CHAIR FOR YOU
YOU'RE GETTING TO BE A REAL GENTLEMAN, HÄGAR
DIK BROWNE
© King Features Syndicate, Inc. World rights reserved.
WELL? WHAT ABOUT MY CHAIR?
ROMANCE IS SHORT LIVED WITH A VIKING

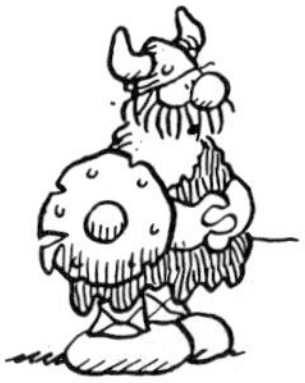

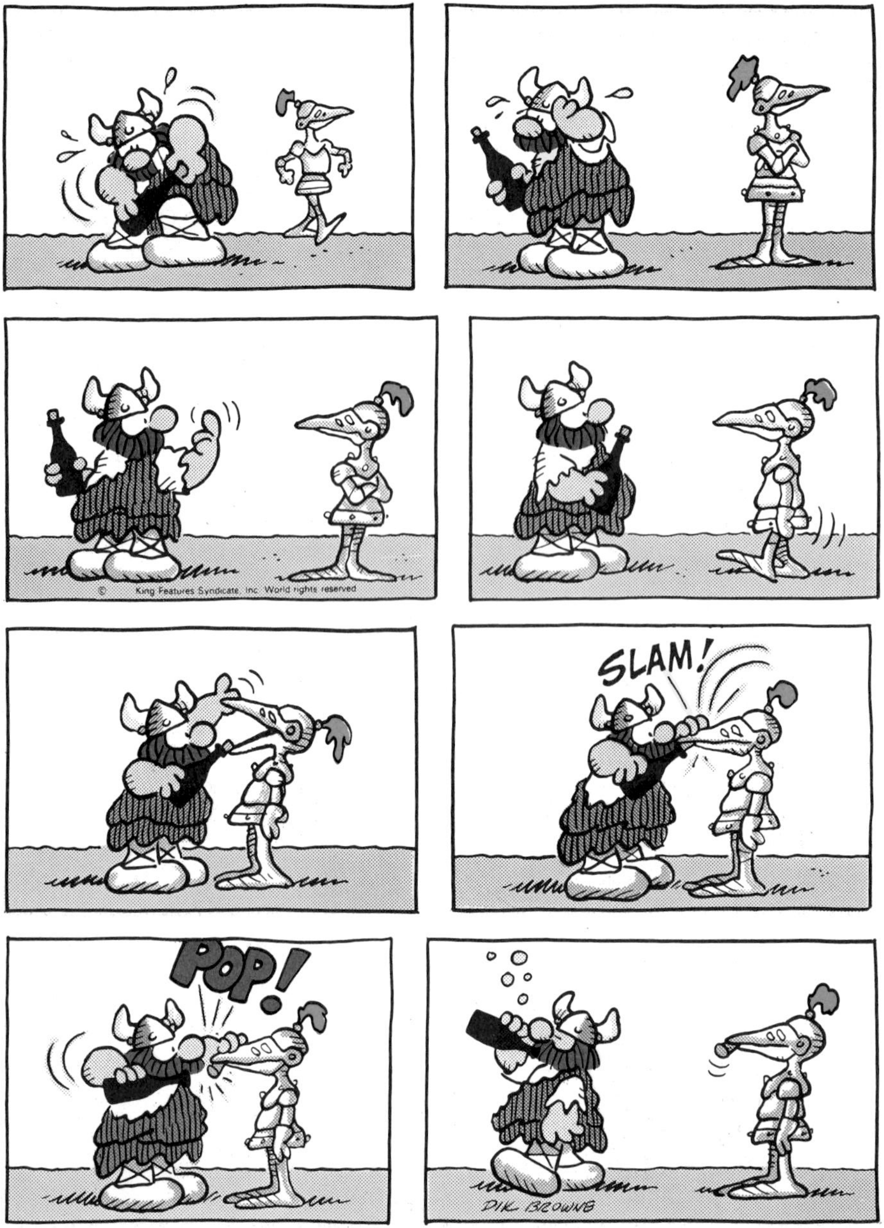
© King Features Syndicate, Inc. World rights reserved
SLAM!
POP!
DIK BROWNE

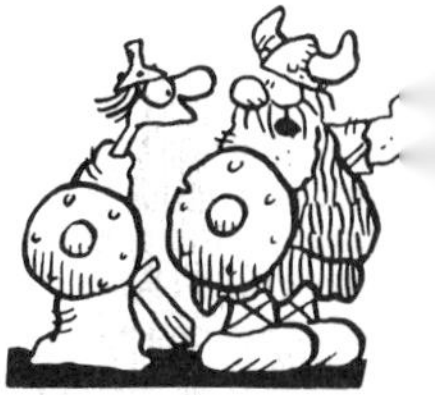

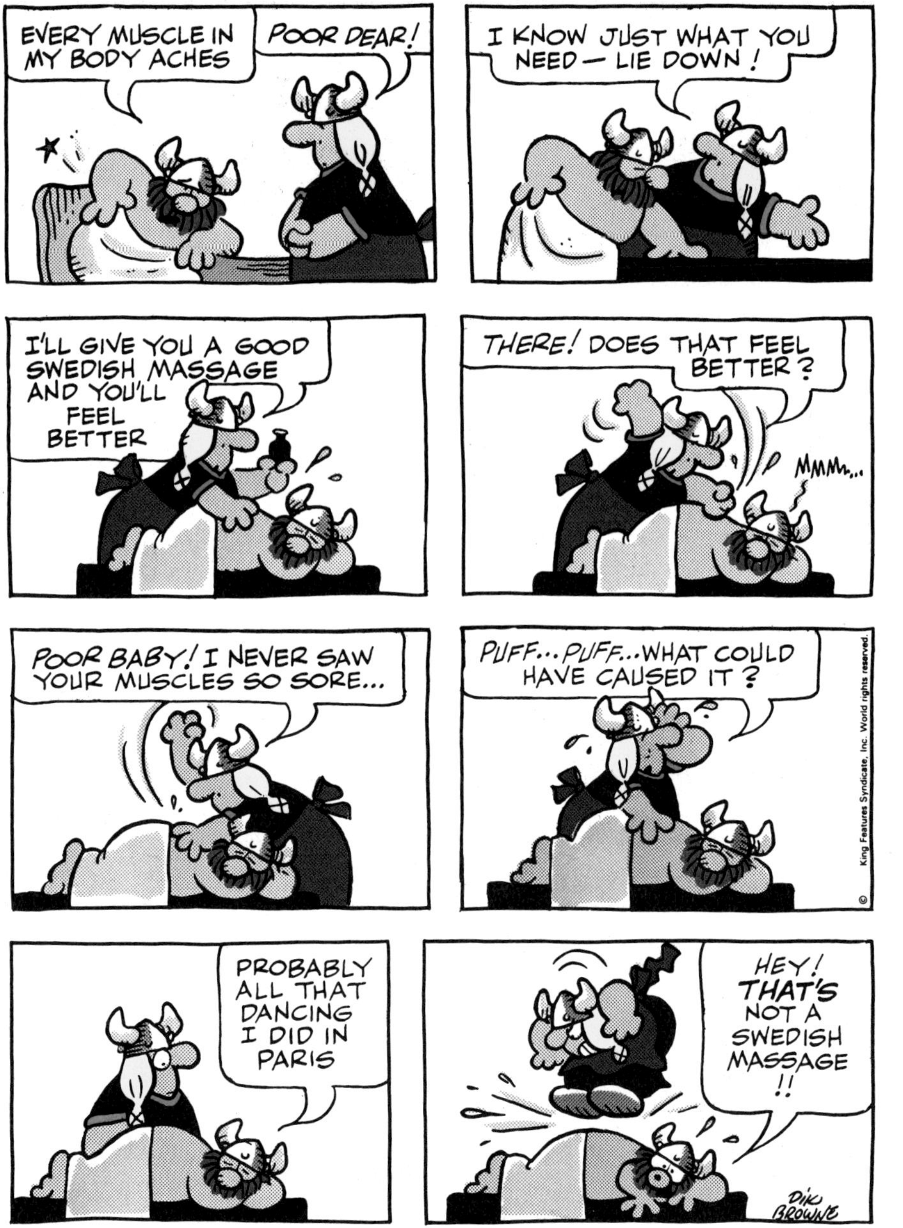
EVERY MUSCLE IN MY BODY ACHES
POOR DEAR!
I KNOW JUST WHAT YOU NEED — LIE DOWN!
I'LL GIVE YOU A GOOD SWEDISH MASSAGE AND YOU'LL FEEL BETTER
THERE! DOES THAT FEEL BETTER?
MMMM...
POOR BABY! I NEVER SAW YOUR MUSCLES SO SORE...
PUFF... PUFF... WHAT COULD HAVE CAUSED IT?
PROBABLY ALL THAT DANCING I DID IN PARIS
HEY! THAT'S NOT A SWEDISH MASSAGE !!
DIK BROWNE

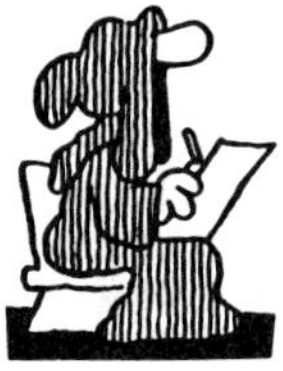

AH!
DIK BROWNE
© King Features Syndicate, Inc. World rights reserved.
AN AFTER-DINNER MINT, SIR?
YEAH!
NOW, DEAR... REMEMBER YOUR DIET
SIGH YES, DEAR

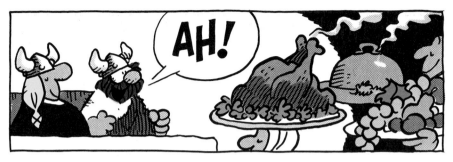

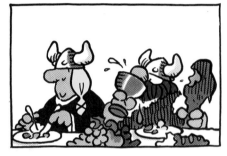

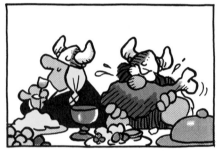

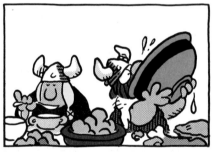

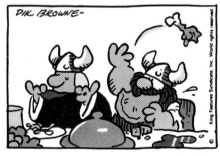

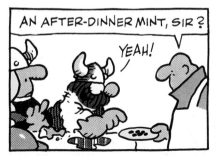

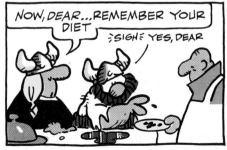

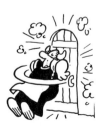

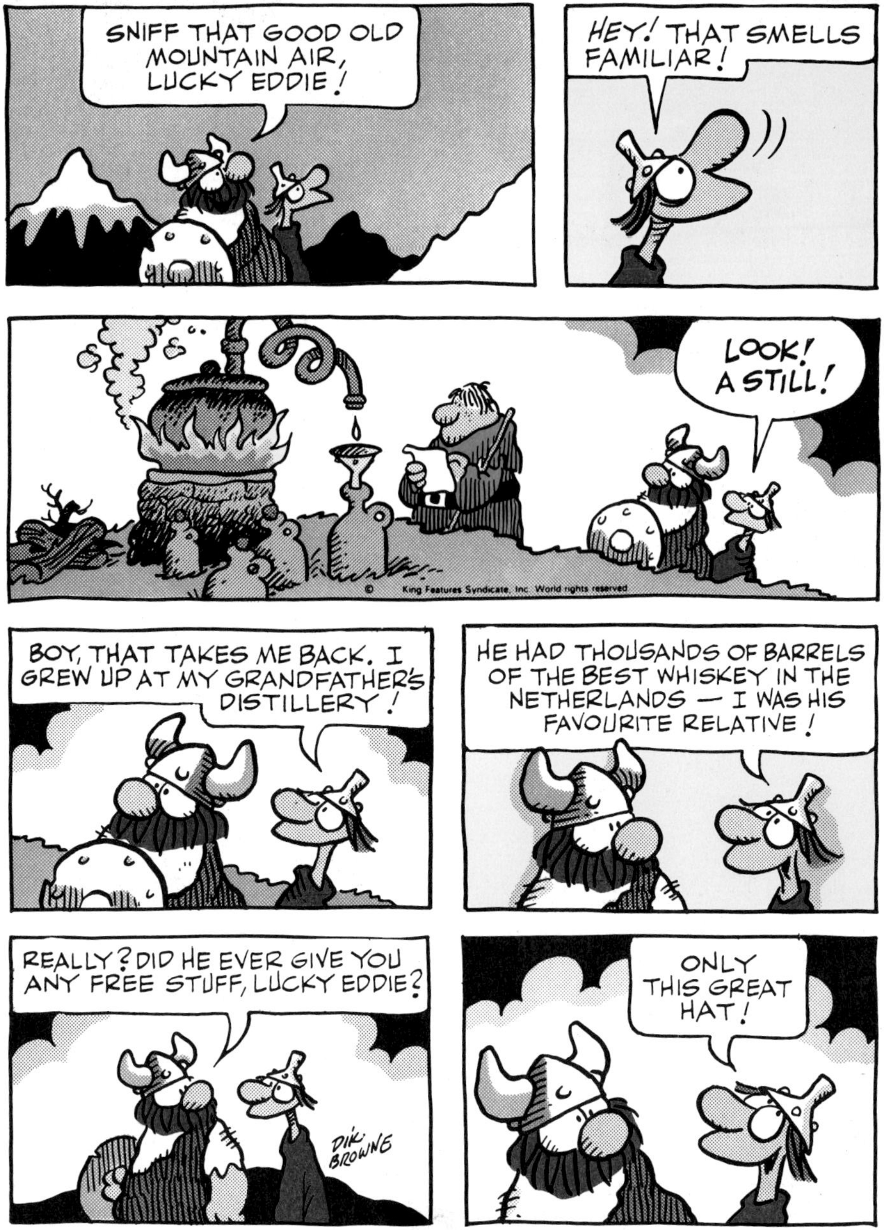
SNIFF THAT GOOD OLD MOUNTAIN AIR, LUCKY EDDIE!
HEY! THAT SMELLS FAMILIAR!
LOOK! A STILL!
© King Features Syndicate, Inc. World rights reserved
BOY, THAT TAKES ME BACK. I GREW UP AT MY GRANDFATHER'S DISTILLERY!
HE HAD THOUSANDS OF BARRELS OF THE BEST WHISKEY IN THE NETHERLANDS — I WAS HIS FAVOURITE RELATIVE!
REALLY? DID HE EVER GIVE YOU ANY FREE STUFF, LUCKY EDDIE?
DIK BROWNE
ONLY THIS GREAT HAT!

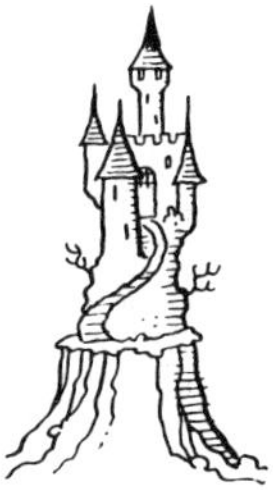

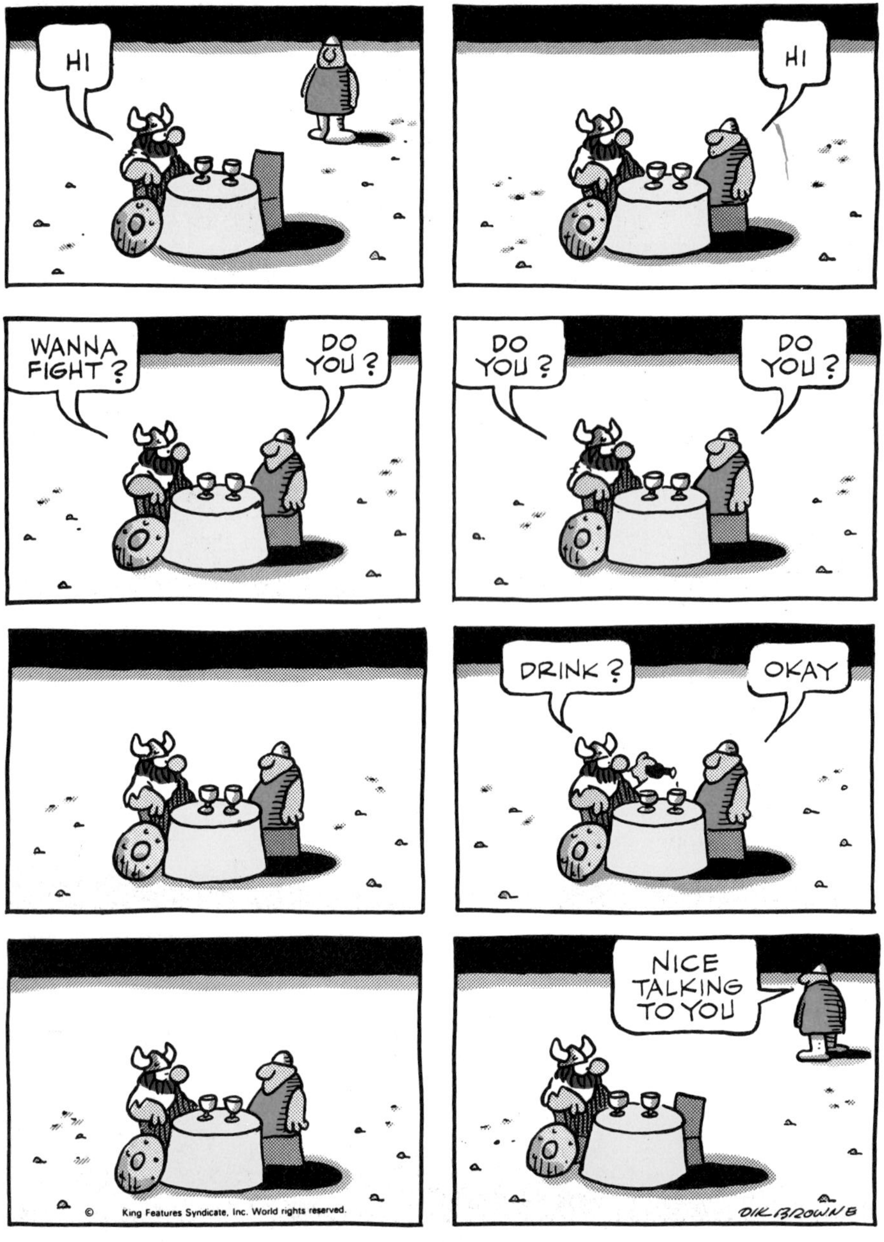
HI
HI
WANNA FIGHT ?
DO YOU ?
DO YOU ?
DO YOU ?
DRINK ?
OKAY
© King Features Syndicate, Inc. World rights reserved.
NICE TALKING TO YOU
DIK BROWNE

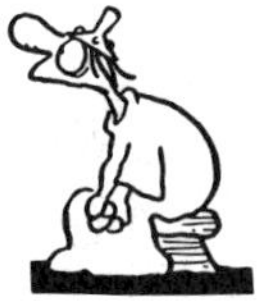

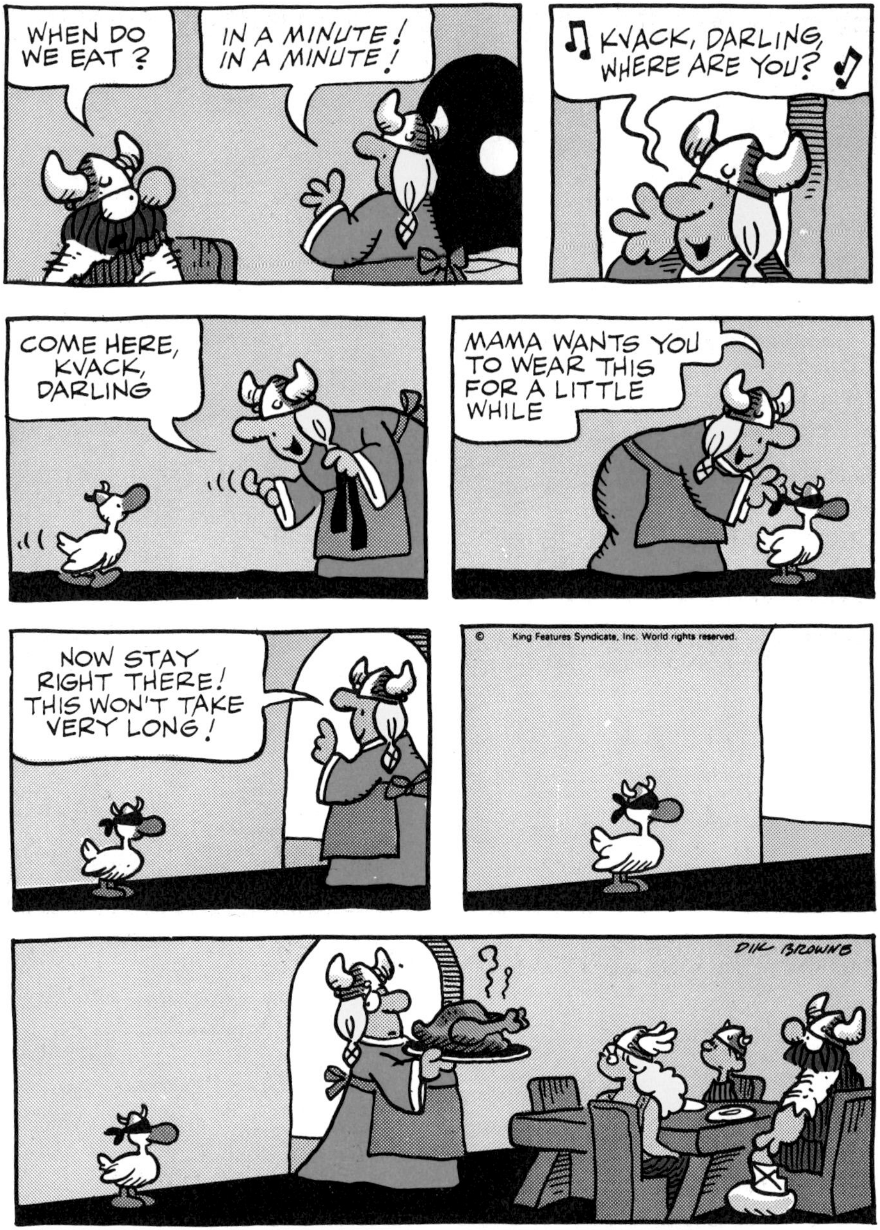
WHEN DO WE EAT ?
IN A MINUTE! IN A MINUTE!
KVACK, DARLING, WHERE ARE YOU?
COME HERE, KVACK, DARLING
MAMA WANTS YOU TO WEAR THIS FOR A LITTLE WHILE
NOW STAY RIGHT THERE! THIS WON'T TAKE VERY LONG!
© King Features Syndicate, Inc. World rights reserved.
DIK BROWNE

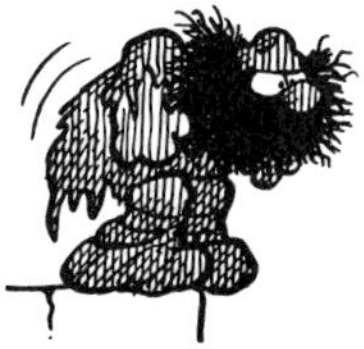

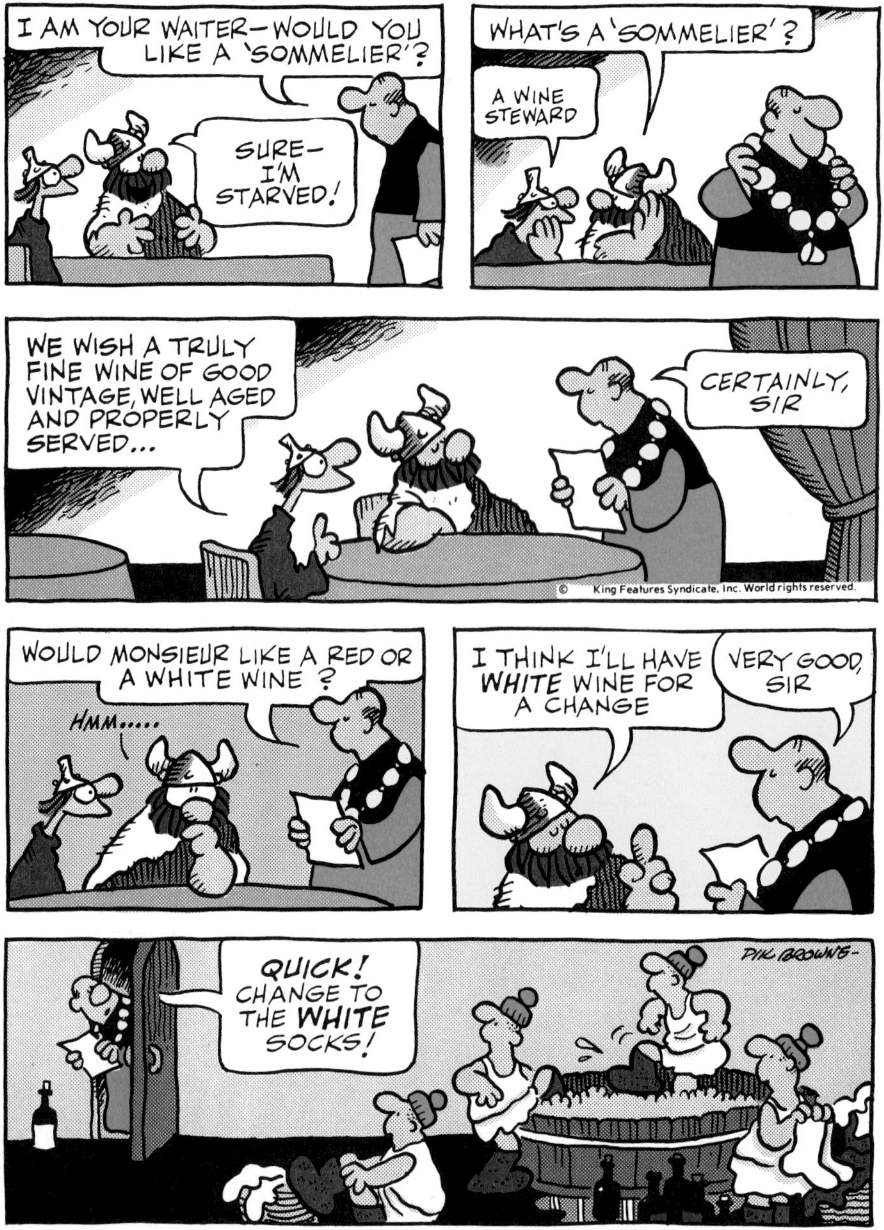

I AM YOUR WAITER—WOULD YOU LIKE A 'SOMMELIER'?
SURE— I'M STARVED!
WHAT'S A 'SOMMELIER'?
A WINE STEWARD
WE WISH A TRULY FINE WINE OF GOOD VINTAGE, WELL AGED AND PROPERLY SERVED...
CERTAINLY, SIR
© King Features Syndicate, Inc. World rights reserved.
WOULD MONSIEUR LIKE A RED OR A WHITE WINE ?
HMM.....
I THINK I'LL HAVE WHITE WINE FOR A CHANGE
VERY GOOD, SIR
QUICK! CHANGE TO THE WHITE SOCKS!
DIK BROWNE-

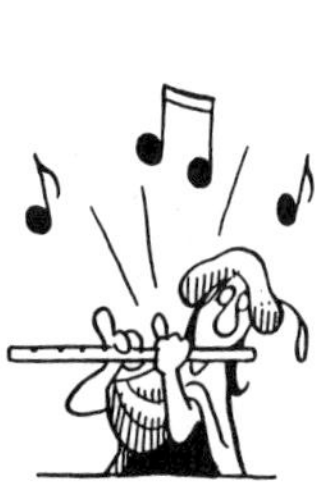

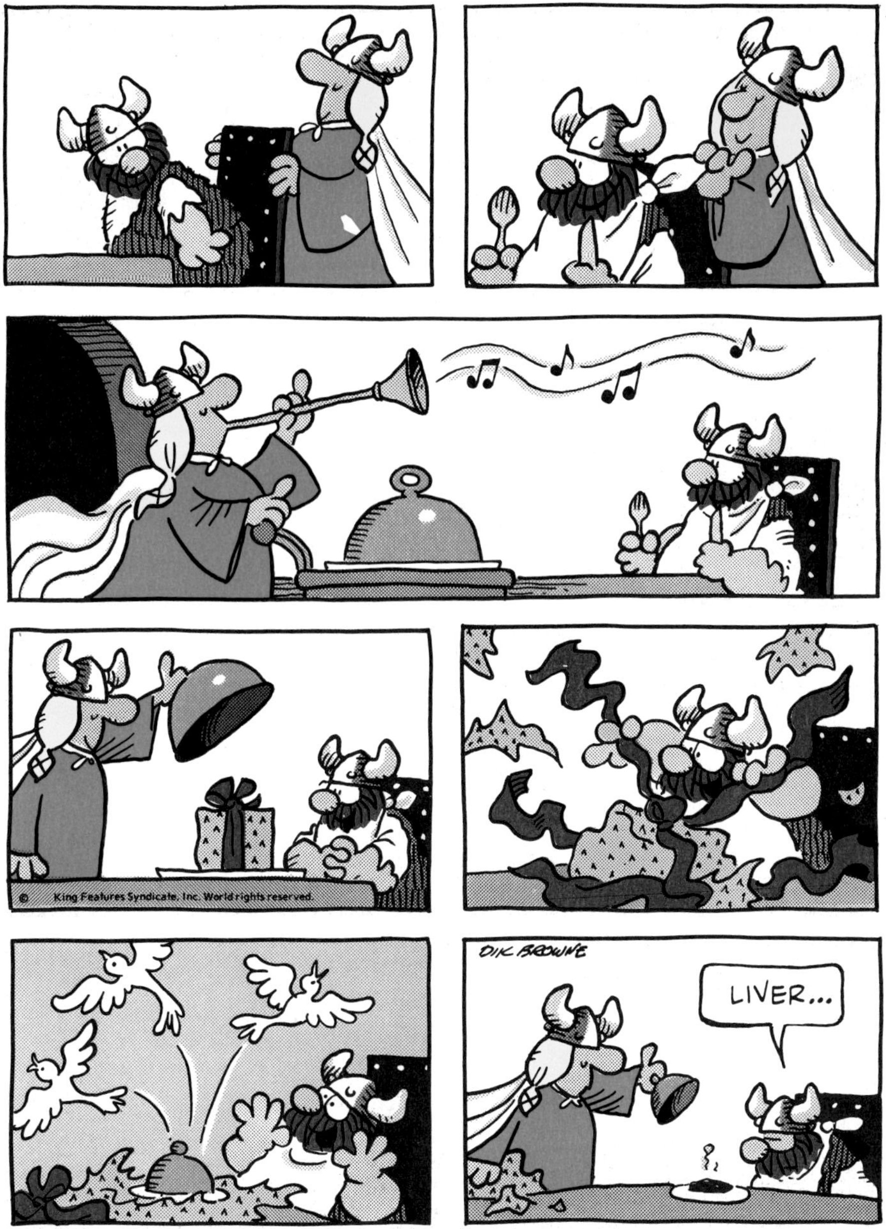
© King Features Syndicate, Inc. World rights reserved.
DIK BROWNE
LIVER...

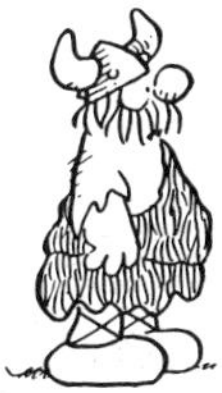

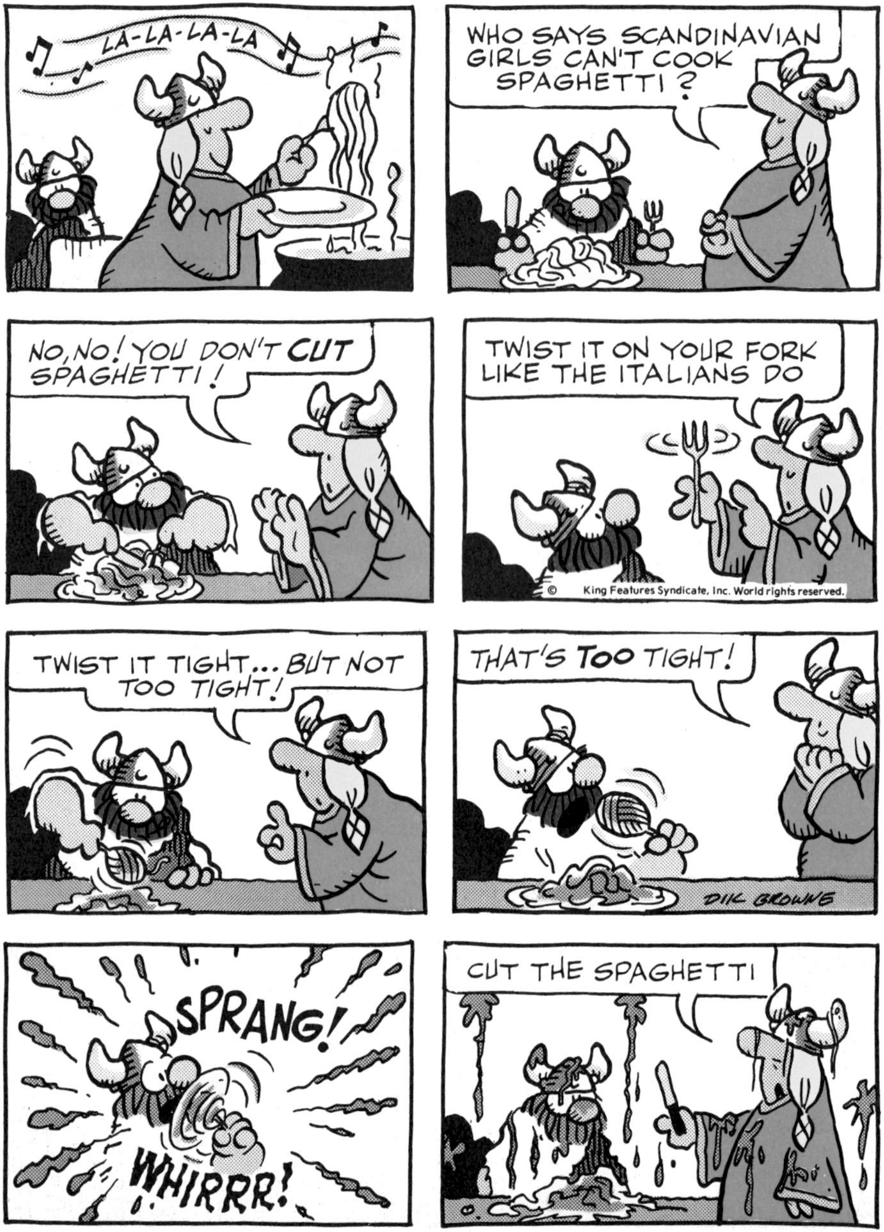

LA-LA-LA-LA
WHO SAYS SCANDINAVIAN GIRLS CAN'T COOK SPAGHETTI ?
NO, NO! YOU DON'T **CUT** SPAGHETTI !
TWIST IT ON YOUR FORK LIKE THE ITALIANS DO
© King Features Syndicate, Inc. World rights reserved.
TWIST IT TIGHT... BUT NOT TOO TIGHT!
THAT'S **TOO** TIGHT!
DIK BROWNE
SPRANG!
WHIRRR!
CUT THE SPAGHETTI

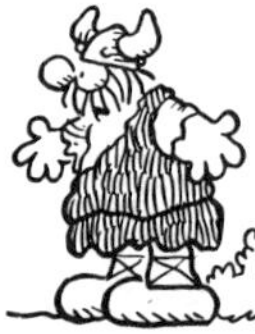

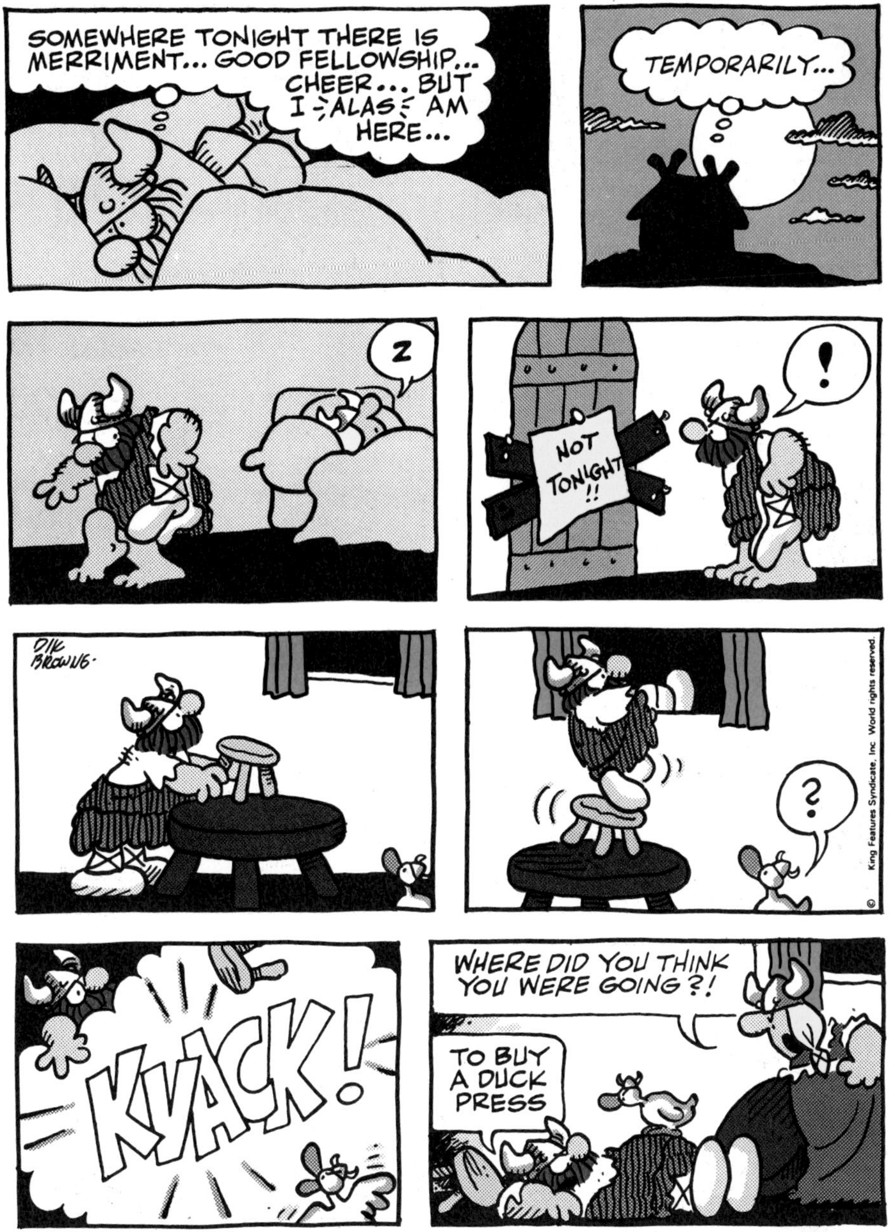
SOMEWHERE TONIGHT THERE IS MERRIMENT... GOOD FELLOWSHIP... CHEER... BUT I -ALAS- AM HERE...
TEMPORARILY...
Z
NOT TONIGHT!!
!
DIK BROWNE
?
© King Features Syndicate, Inc. World rights reserved.
KYACK!
WHERE DID YOU THINK YOU WERE GOING?!
TO BUY A DUCK PRESS

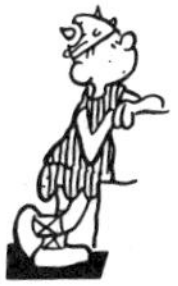

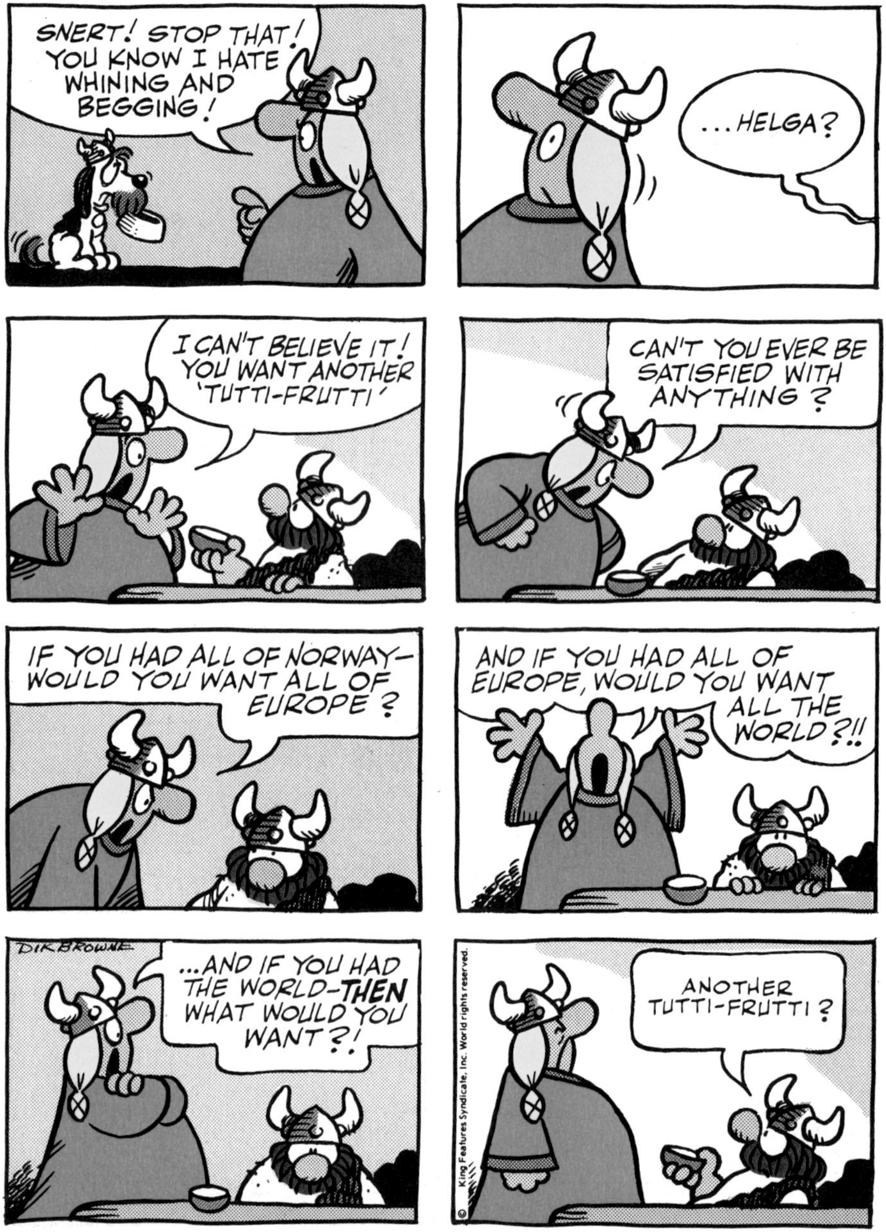
SNERT! STOP THAT! YOU KNOW I HATE WHINING AND BEGGING!
...HELGA?
I CAN'T BELIEVE IT! YOU WANT ANOTHER 'TUTTI-FRUTTI'
CAN'T YOU EVER BE SATISFIED WITH ANYTHING?
IF YOU HAD ALL OF NORWAY- WOULD YOU WANT ALL OF EUROPE?
AND IF YOU HAD ALL OF EUROPE, WOULD YOU WANT ALL THE WORLD?!!
DIK BROWNE
...AND IF YOU HAD THE WORLD-THEN WHAT WOULD YOU WANT?!
© King Features Syndicate, Inc. World rights reserved.
ANOTHER TUTTI-FRUTTI?

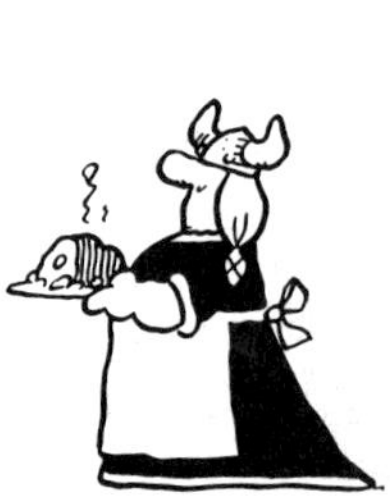

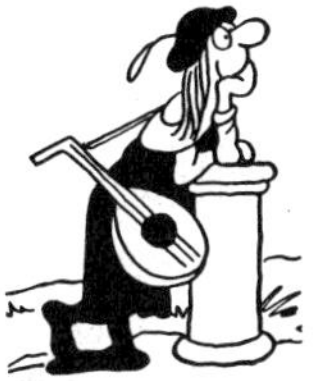

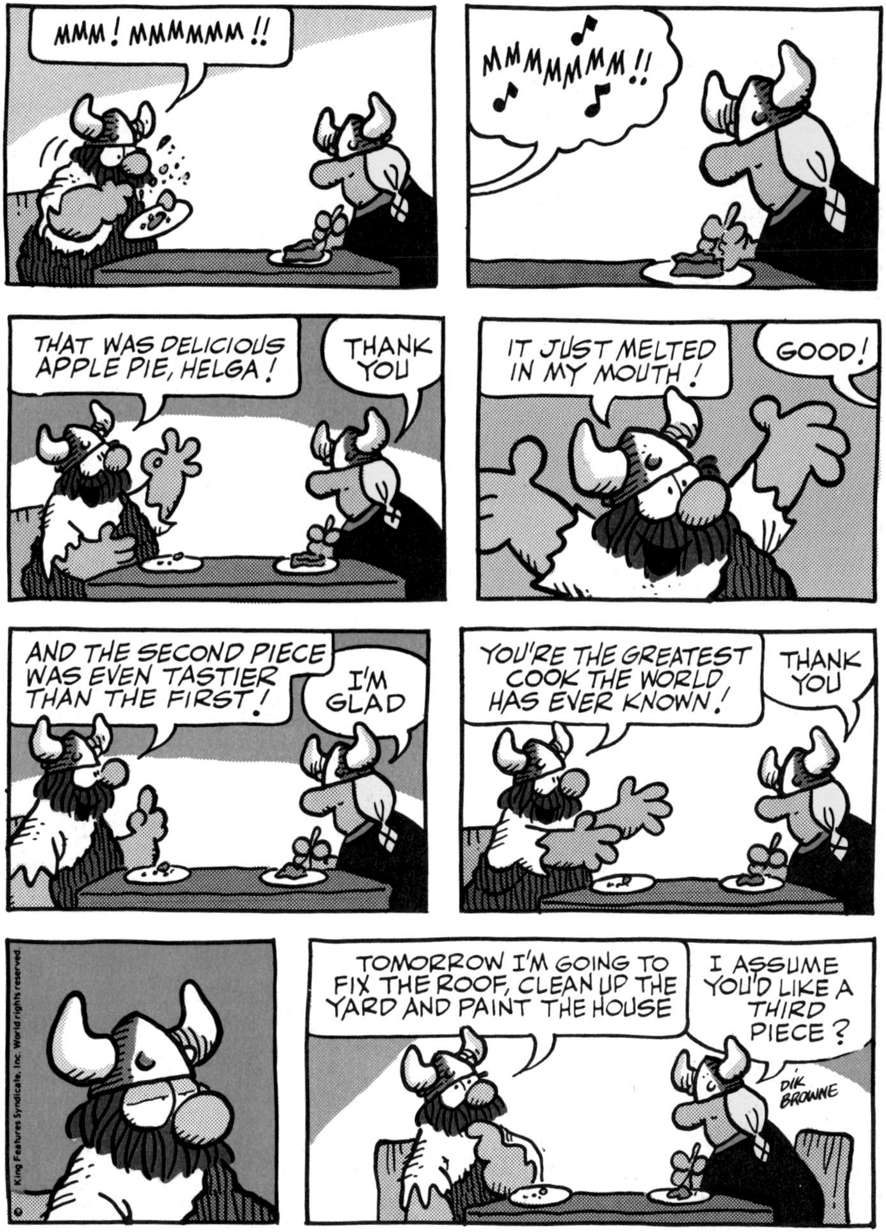
MMM! MMMMMM!!
MMMMMMM!!
THAT WAS DELICIOUS APPLE PIE, HELGA!
THANK YOU
IT JUST MELTED IN MY MOUTH!
GOOD!
AND THE SECOND PIECE WAS EVEN TASTIER THAN THE FIRST!
I'M GLAD
YOU'RE THE GREATEST COOK THE WORLD HAS EVER KNOWN!
THANK YOU
© King Features Syndicate, Inc. World rights reserved.
TOMORROW I'M GOING TO FIX THE ROOF, CLEAN UP THE YARD AND PAINT THE HOUSE
I ASSUME YOU'D LIKE A THIRD PIECE?
DIK BROWNE

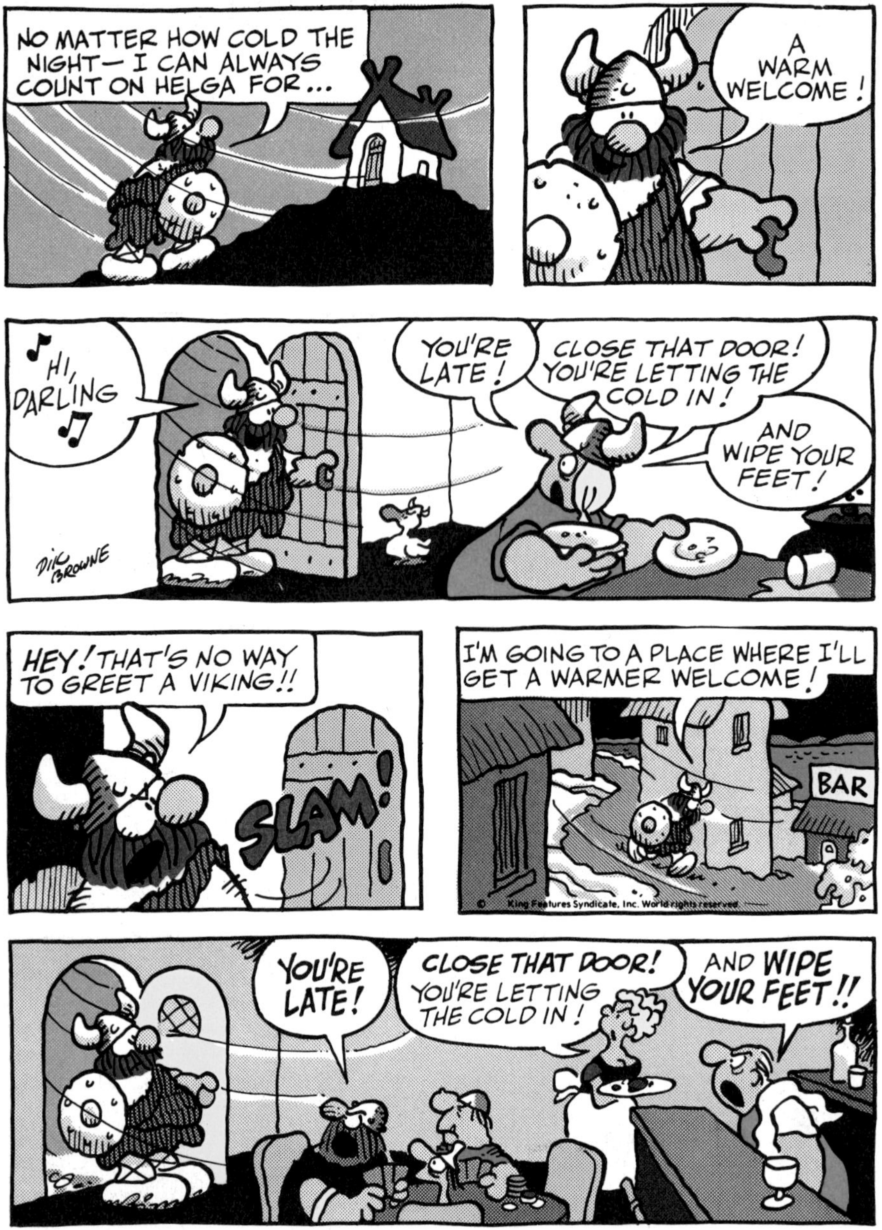
NO MATTER HOW COLD THE NIGHT— I CAN ALWAYS COUNT ON HELGA FOR...
A WARM WELCOME!
HI, DARLING
YOU'RE LATE!
CLOSE THAT DOOR! YOU'RE LETTING THE COLD IN!
AND WIPE YOUR FEET!
DIK BROWNE
HEY! THAT'S NO WAY TO GREET A VIKING!!
SLAM!
I'M GOING TO A PLACE WHERE I'LL GET A WARMER WELCOME!
BAR
© King Features Syndicate, Inc. World rights reserved.
YOU'RE LATE!
CLOSE THAT DOOR! YOU'RE LETTING THE COLD IN!
AND WIPE YOUR FEET!!

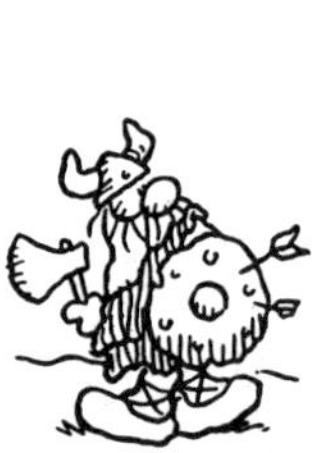

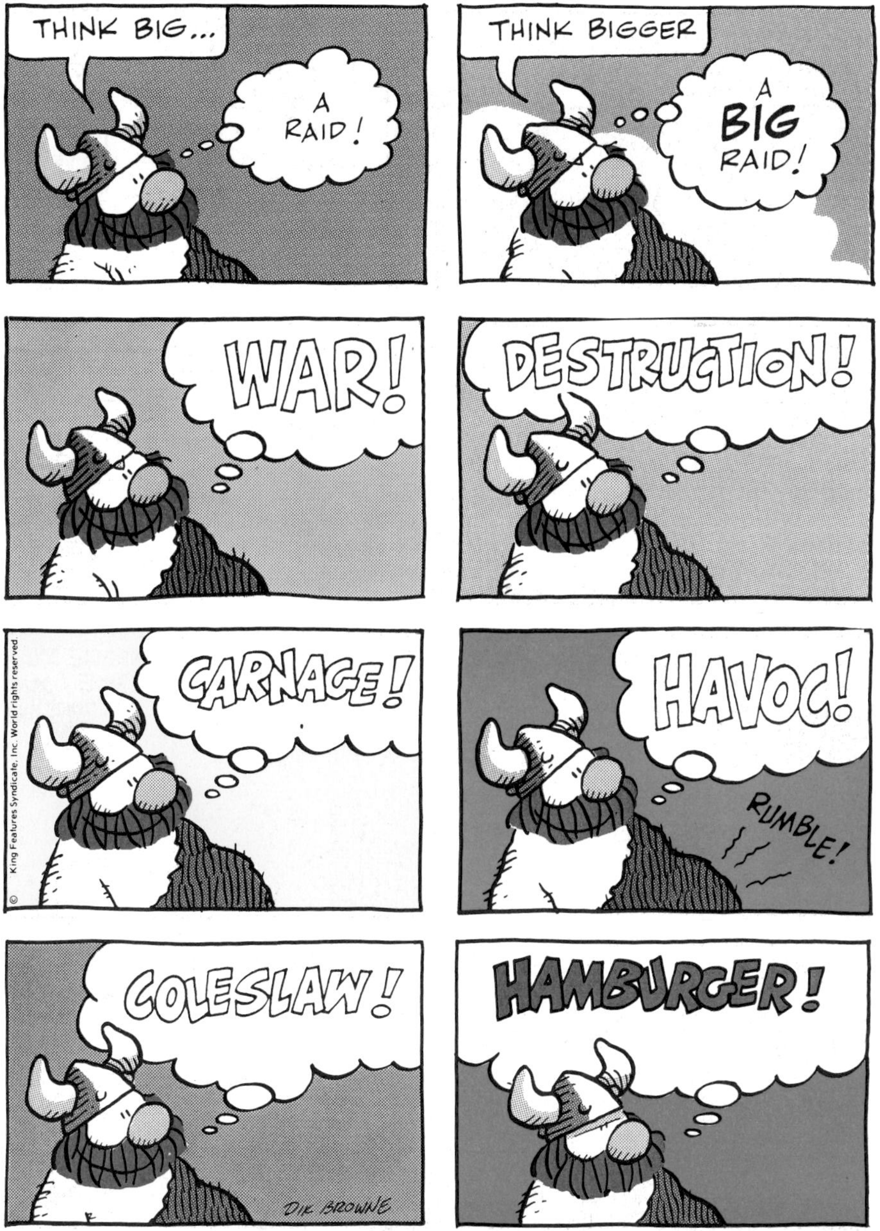
THINK BIG...
A RAID!
THINK BIGGER
A BIG RAID!
WAR!
DESTRUCTION!
CARNAGE!
HAVOC!
RUMBLE!
COLESLAW!
HAMBURGER!
DIK BROWNE

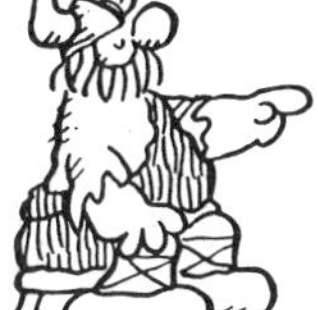

A selection of HÄGAR books published by Ravette

COLOUR THEME BOOKS *£2.95 each*
No 2 TROUBLE AND STRIFE
No 3 TAKES A JOURNEY
No 4 WHO DARES WINS
No 5 CHILD'S PLAY

POCKET BOOKS *£1.95 each*
TRIES AGAIN
HAS A GO
IN A FIX
ON THE RAMPAGE
GETS IT ALL
IN THE ROUGH
LEADS THE WAY
TAKES A BREAK
ALL AT SEA
ON HOLIDAY
TAKES AIM
IN A STEW

ALBUMS *£2.50 each*
THE HERO
LETS HIMSELF GO

BLACK AND WHITE LANDSCAPES *£2.50 each*
MEETS HIS MATCH
IN A HURRY

COLOUR LANDSCAPES *£2.95 each*
TELLS IT LIKE IT IS
NEVER SAY DIE
MAKES AN ENTRANCE
WELCOME HOME

VIKING HANDBOOK *£3.95*

All these books are available at your local bookshop or newsagent, or can be ordered direct from the publisher. Just tick the titles you require and fill in the form below. Prices and availability subject to change without notice.

Ravette Books Limited, 3 Glenside Estate, Star Road, Partridge Green, Horsham, West Sussex RH13 8RA

Please send a cheque or postal order and allow the following for postage and packing. UK: Pocket books – 45p for one book plus 20p for the second book and 15p for each additional book. Landscape series – 50p for one book plus 30p for each additional book. Other titles – 85p for one book plus 60p for each additional book.

Name ....

Address ....

....